Alaska's
Inside Passage

Ann Chandonnet
Photography by Don Pitcher

COMPASS AMERICAN GUIDES
An imprint of Fodor's Travel

Compass American Guides: Alaska's Inside Passage

Compass Senior Editor: Jennifer Paull
Editor: Emmanuelle Alspaugh
Designers: Chie Ushio, Tigist Getachew
Cover Design: Nora Rosansky
Compass Creative Director: Fabrizio La Rocca
Production Editor: Astrid deRidder
Photo Editor and Archival Researcher: Melanie Marin
Map Design: Mark Stroud, Moon Street Cartography
Production Manager: Angela L. McLean

Cover photo: Don Pitcher

Second Edition
ISBN 978–1–4000–0902–2
ISSN 1559–0828

The details in this book are based on information supplied to us at press time, but changes occur all the time, and the publisher cannot accept responsibility for facts that become outdated or for inadvertent errors or omissions.

This book is available at special discounts for bulk purchases for sales promotions or premiums. Special editions, including personalized covers, excerpts of existing books, and corporate imprints, can be created in large quantities for special needs. For more information, write to Special Markets/Premium Sales. 1745 Broadway, MD 6-2, New York, New York 10019, or e-mail specialmarkets@randomhouse.com.

Compass American Guides, 1745 Broadway, New York, NY 10019

PRINTED IN CHINA

10 9 8 7 6 5 4 3 2

*To the memory
of my dear "Gram,"
who always wanted
to see Alaska.*

C O N T E N T S

INTRODUCTION 9
How to Use This Book 14

THE LAND AND THE PEOPLE 17
A Rare Rain Forest 17
The Glaciers 18
Native Alaskans 19
Native Traditions............................ 21
The Explorers' Impact..................... 23
New Claims to Southeast Alaska 25

KETCHIKAN 30
WRANGELL 50
PETERSBURG..............................69
JUNEAU 83
SKAGWAY................................. 117
HAINES 133
GLACIER BAY NATIONAL PARK
AND PRESERVE......................... 153
SITKA 162

PRACTICAL INFORMATION... 180
Animal- and Bird-Watching............ 180
Animal Safety................................ 182
Antiquities Laws............................ 183
Boating 184
Climate 185
Clothing....................................... 185
Festivals and Annual Events............ 186
Fishing 189
Flightseeing.................................. 190
Food... 190
Getting Around............................. 191
Gold Panning................................ 192
Green Travel: Bike Tours 193
Lodging and Camping 193
Shopping Tips 194
Survival 195
Time 195
Traveling with Kids 196
Useful Contacts............................. 196

RECOMMENDED READING ... 200
Index.. 202

SIDEBARS

Glacier Facts.. 19
Misty Fiords 42
Early Inside Passage Cruises.. 44
Totem Poles... 59
Basics on Bears 62-63
Of Flippers and Flukes 75
Tracing Juneau's Gold Belt 87
Lighthouses 93
Roots Travel: Finding Great-Granddad... 97
Treadwell Past and Present.. 111
Hubbard Glacier 130
Let the Mask Buyer Beware 141
Eagles and Ravens 147
A Tlingit Sampler... 172
The Tongass... 177

LITERARY EXTRACTS

John Muir *on the Inside Passage's landscape*..................................... 23
George F. MacDonald *on the Haida world.* 35
Chief Toyatte *speaking on behalf of the Stickeen people*....................... 55
Michael Modzelewski *on forest hiking* 78
Earl Redman *on the Gold Rush's "amalgam thieves"*........................... 89
Harry M. Walker *on the Mendenhall Glacier* 103
Martha Black *on braving the Chilkoot Trail*................................... 122
Paul Alaback *on the Tongass National Forest* 138
Gretel Ehrlich *on glaciers as archivists* 156
Victoria Wyatt *on the influence of missionaries and
businessmen on Native culture* 167

MAPS

Upper Southeast 11

Lower Southeast 15

Ketchikan 32

Wrangell 52

Petersburg 71

Greater Juneau 85

Downtown Juneau 88

Skagway 119

Haines 137

Glacier Bay National Park and Preserve 154

Sitka 164

INTRODUCTION

The mesmerizing effects of light on water, quickly changing skies, rocky promontories, thundering cataracts, silvery mists, dense foliage. Get set for a sensory immersion in nature's splendor.

If the painters of the 19th-century Hudson River school could have cruised along Alaska's Inside Passage they would have thought they'd died and gone to artists' heaven. Enraptured as they were with the American wilderness, imagine how they would have reacted to the Alaskan landscape, which makes the Catskill Mountains look like Central Park. The Hudson River school painters believed art capable of moral and spiritual transformation. Alaskans believe nature has those abilities.

Europeans discovered Alaska when a Russian expedition sighted the territory in 1741. The name "Alaska" comes from the Aleut word *alyeska*, meaning "Great Land." The Russians began their incursions in the Aleutians and Commander Islands. Wherever the *promyshlenniki* (fur hunters-traders) could not easily obtain sea-otter pelts themselves, they forced the Aleuts to hunt for them. Gradually they explored eastward. Within 20 years the *promyshlenniki* reached Kodiak Island, enslaving Native Alaskans as they went. When Aleksandr Baranov became the chief manager of the Russian-American Company, he expanded operations south, establishing a permanent post at Sitka in 1804. The Native Tlingits, uneasy about their occupiers, often fought back. Only a continent-wide smallpox epidemic in the late 1830s finally quashed their resistance.

In the meantime, the southernmost part of Alaska—the 500-mile-long, curved, lush coastal strip called the Panhandle—had become its best-known region. This area had milder winters than the Arctic and was easily accessible from major ports like San Francisco, Seattle, Port Townsend, and Vancouver. Steamships began to carry tourists to the Panhandle's scenic waterways in the 1880s. The Klondike Gold Rush of 1896–98 further piqued the tourists' curiosity. The Inside Passage was one of the main routes to the Klondike gold fields, and after stampeders had blazed the trail, more and more tourists ventured north on summer steamship jaunts. They clicked new portable Kodak cameras to record their scenic adventures.

The Coast Mountains from the backdrop for Haines's Portage Cove.

With this Treasury Warrant, the U.S. snapped up Alaska for two cents an acre.

In the Inside Passage's winding waterway, 1,500 islands act as bulwarks against large surges from the open Pacific. When a storm rages in the exposed Gulf of Alaska, for example, creating 11-foot seas, the seas in sheltered Stephens Passage may measure a calmer 4 feet.

The phrase "Inside Passage" came into use in 1885, when Lieutenant Commander Richardson Clover USN used it to indicate the saltwater passage connecting Tongass Narrow and Clarence Strait. However, it quickly came to mean all the passages between Sitkian Island and Disenchantment Bay. And sometimes the phrase is used for the passages just north of Vancouver.

The best way to get to know Alaska may be to corner an Alaskan—not a Sourdough-come-lately who visits annually for the salmon derbies but somebody who's struggled through a dozen winters and can still grin.

Likely as not, that person will start his or her story with, "I didn't intend to stay . . ." and proceed from there. Women come with their husbands' jobs. Men come with military service or oil companies. It's "a year or two and we'll see."

Then somebody buys a rifle for caribou, the second car parks in the driveway because of an avalanche of camping gear, a resident fishing license looks better and better, studded tires become old friends, the used boat ads get a lot of scanning. In other words, Alaska gets inside you and becomes home.

Alaska has no "tales of the city." We chuckle when a visitor asks for a map of the state, looks it over, and quickly hands it back, shaking his head, asking,

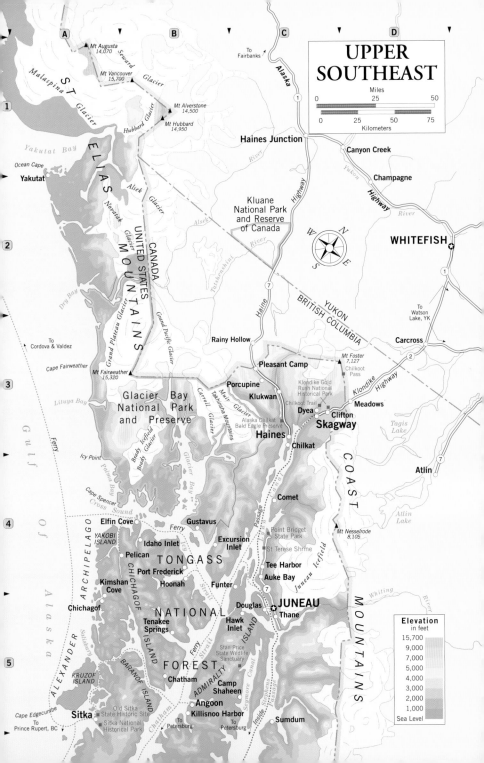

The Point Retreat
lighthouse toughs
it out on Admiralty
Island, near Juneau.

"Where are the roads?" It's true, paved highways are few and far between here, but don't let that stop you. Living along the Inside Passage, I came to appreciate the Norse phrase for the open sea, "the whale road." Once you've seen killer whales flashing across the surface or humpbacks giving a saucy wave of their flukes, the phrase takes on a fresh, dramatic meaning.

Walk across the wetlands of Gustavus in May and relish the pleasure of striding knee-deep through chocolate lilies, violet-blue lupine, and hot pink shooting stars. Dive into a remote lake and see if the loons will swim up to inspect you. Get down on your knees to greet a Calypso orchid face-to-face. Lean against an ancient trunk and listen for woodpeckers. Pull in a struggling halibut you think you can't pull in. Look for moose as you soar in a six-seater Piper Cherokee.

After more than 30 years in Alaska, I found that some of the best times are to be had on foot, in a kayak, standing at the rail of a ferry or excursion vessel, or exploring back roads. Come and see for yourself. You won't be sorry.

HOW TO USE THIS BOOK

The chapters are arranged in order of a fantasy cruise from south to north with a fishhook loop near the end: Ketchikan, Wrangell, Petersburg, Juneau, Skagway, Haines, Glacier Bay, and Sitka.

A site map shows the locations of historic buildings, museums, totems, harbors, monuments, and other points of interest in each city or town.

Each chapter kicks off with frequently asked questions (FAQs).

Kid Stuff sections suggest activities that appeal to children—some participatory, some as observers. (Note: Children should always be accompanied by an adult.)

Each town chapter includes a walking tour of moderate length. These walks are laid out in an easily followed, point-to-point manner.

Each town chapter also includes Brief Excursions and Longer Outings sections. Listings in Brief Excursions cover local sights and activities that can be enjoyed in an hour to three hours—anything from a short hike or tour of a museum to a Tlingit canoe-carving workshop. Longer Outings point you to side trips that take anywhere from four hours to several days. Dining and shopping suggestions are also included for each town.

Finally, the comprehensive index includes activities, festivals, historical figures, and attractions. Venues that are accessible to travelers with limited mobility are indexed under "accessible."

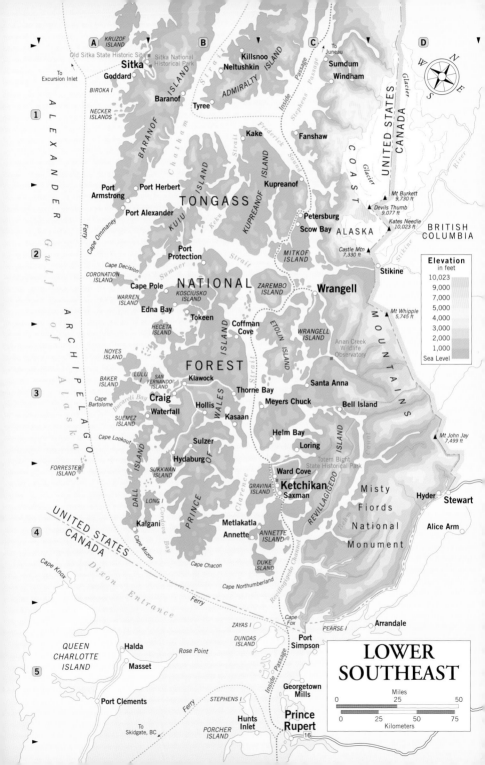

LOWER
SOUTHEAST

A Tlingit man and woman pose in traditional dancing costumes, ca. 1906.

THE LAND
AND THE PEOPLE

The steep wooded hills, icy glaciers, drenched forests, and narrow shoreline of southeast Alaska have so shaped the cultures here that it is difficult to consider habitat and residents separately.

"Land is the simplest form of architecture," Frank Lloyd Wright wrote. Everywhere along the Inside Passage, veils of shifting mist glide up steep ravines of dark spruce like animated chalk drawings. At high tide, martens dogpaddle along the shore, plucking mussels from rocks. In dozens of small harbors, boats tug at their lines like young stallions ready for a gallop. Mating bald eagles join talons and free-fall, spinning wildly, each daring the other to let go.

Once this dance was staged above and in my Juneau backyard. I was weeding daylilies when two eagles fell into the adjoining patch of woods. Neither would admit to being "chicken," so the pair plummeted right into the dense spruce and alder "hells." One managed to rise again, but the chagrined second had to walk awkwardly out into the daylight of my rhubarb patch in order to take to the sky.

Southeast Alaska is chiefly a land of mild, even temperatures and heavy rainfall. The water falls from evergreen needle to leaf to sphagnum, and then seeps through thin acid soils. Murmuring spruce and hemlocks, cedars, and yews flourish in dense stands from water's edge to tree line. Some trees soar more than a hundred feet into the air. Meanwhile the forest floor is a tangle of alder, blueberry, prickly rose, thorny devil's club, ferns, mosses, Deer Heart, and skunk cabbage. Uncountable creeks wend their way through the land, occasionally crisscrossed with giant trunks felled by the wind, their exposed root systems the height of a garage. Sitka black-tailed deer, shrews, bears, red-breasted sapsuckers, and flying squirrels inhabit these forests.

A RARE RAIN FOREST

Alaska's rain forest is the northern portion of a continuous forest pressed against the warm vapors of the ocean currents and guarded from the interior's freezing temperatures by the Pacific Coast Ranges. Old-growth temperate rain forest like this is the rarest forest type on earth—much rarer than tropical rain forest.

This unique habitat, capable of producing swamps on steep slopes, stretches from Yakutat to Seattle. Some biogeographers contend that the rain forest extends far beyond the Inside Passage—all the way from Kodiak Island to Monterey, California. The western hemlock and Sitka spruce forest spreads its verdant branches from Oregon to Prince William Sound. National borders scissor this mighty arc, but it remains an ecological whole. Both British Columbia and downtown Juneau are sopped with an average annual rainfall of 100 inches.

Temperate rain forest means jaw-dropping scenery at every bend in the trail. It means lush, undeveloped land, and 50 shades of luminous green.

THE GLACIERS

At the height of the Wisconsin glaciation, about 20,000 years ago, things were different. Most of southeast Alaska was covered by an undulating plain of ice so thick that only mountain peaks higher than 5,000 feet pierced through. As the glaciers advanced and retreated, their grinding and polishing slowly carved out U-shaped valleys. Where they opened to the sea they created magnificent fjords rivaled only by those of Norway—the fjords that would later beckon to explorers.

About 12,000 years ago the climate began to change, and V-shaped valleys were dug out by streams, rivers, and landslides. After another 4,000 years the land began to rise, lifting areas like the Mendenhall Flats above sea level. Tectonic forces have also raised parts of the Inside Passage, although it is less subject to seismic temblors than Kodiak or San Francisco.

As glaciers recede, living things colonize the exposed raw rock in a particular succession. First, mosquitoes deposit their larvae in melt puddles. Next, breezes carry spores of mosses or the parachute-equipped seeds of fireweed. Other seeds are dropped by birds. These grow and pave the way for more plant life. After about a decade, new homesteaders arrive: horsetails, mountain avens, and lichens. Creatures on the scene vary from hover flies to Dolly Varden char, sticklebacks, nervous shrews, and blustering wolverines. The glacier's blue tongue melts away, leaving a spoor of damp rubble. After another 25 years thriving alder and willow thickets take root in this rubble. These pioneer shrubs fix nitrogen and create soil, in turn allowing a mixed spruce and black cottonwood forest to flourish a mere century after the tongue of ice withdrew.

Although British Columbia and Cape Cod have not felt the weight of large glaciers for 10,000 years, southeast Alaska shook hands with the Little Ice Age about 2,000 years ago. In places like Glacier Bay, advancing glaciers reached their maximum forward thrust as recently as the mid-1700s. Since then most Inside Passage glaciers have receded.

GLACIER FACTS

- Alaska has more active glaciers than the rest of the inhabited world combined, covering huge swatches of the Southeast's St. Elias and Coast Mountains. Three percent of Alaska is under ice.

- Glaciers are made up of ancient, condensed snow. When snowflakes fall, they are 80 percent air. As snow layers accumulate, the flakes compress into rounded grains. Additional weight from each year's snowfall slowly presses these grains into blue ice with less than 20 percent air content. It can take centuries to compress snow into sparkling jewels like the Malaspina or LeConte glaciers.

- Glaciers advance on a layer of meltwater that can be as thin as a sheet of paper.

- As a result of global warming, temperatures near Mendenhall Glacier have risen 5 degrees F since the 1930s, melting the face back one and a half miles.

NATIVE ALASKANS

With the land so difficult to cross, early peoples used glaciers as frozen portages, and kept to routes where rivers gave access to the backcountry. The ocean waterways, except along the outer coast, are protected from the sea's breakers, so Pacific Northwest peoples could easily row their canoes on the gentle swells.

The wet weather and harsh terrain might make the place seem uninhabitable until you consider its wealth of fish, berries, furs, marine mammals, shellfish, waterfowl, copper, wood, and fresh water. With this bounty close at hand, man could easily preserve foodstuffs for the winter, allowing ample leisure for storytelling, celebration, and art. It was this combination of resources and leisure that attracted and held the coastal Indians living north of Washington State: the Salish, Nootka, Kwakiutl, Bella Coola, Haida, Tsimshian, and Tlingit. These peoples survived in isolation for centuries, developing distinctive institutions and patterns of behavior. (The Salish, Nootka, Kwakiutl, and Bella Coola reside in Canadian territory and, although related to the Haida, Tsimshian, and Tlingit, will not be discussed here.)

Each people harvested a broad territory. The Haida (pronounced *high-dah*) lived on the Queen Charlotte Islands and the southern part of Prince of Wales Island. They were renowned for the size and excellence of their cedar canoes. The Tsimshian (*sim-shee-ahn*) claimed fishing camps on the lower Skeena River and hooligan fishing grounds on the lower Nass. They took advantage of seasonal foods by efficiently drying and smoking fish and meat, rendering oil from fish and seals, and preserving berries and wild crab apples in oil. The Tlingit (*kling-git*) occupied the largest territory, the coast from Yakutat Bay to Cape Fox. Like the Tsimshian, the Tlingit lived in plank houses during the winter. They built smoke-houses and lean-tos covered with bark or mats at hunting and fishing sites.

How large were these populations? That's difficult to say. A survey of the Tlingit made in 1839 for the Hudson's Bay Company, taken after a smallpox epidemic had raged for three years, and not including Sitka or the settlements from the Alsek River to Controller Bay, counted a population of 5,455 "Kolosh" (as the Russians called them). In 1967 the Bureau of Indian Affairs counted 320 Haida

Haida dancers in potlatch regalia.

living in the villages of Craig and Hydaburg and 8,482 Tlingit. The BIA estimated that "considerable numbers" of Alaskan Natives were living in Anchorage, Seattle, and Oakland, California, "where chance for employment is greater."

NATIVE TRADITIONS

Each Native people, the Haida, Tsimshian, and Tlingit, was divided into groups of clans called moieties. The Tsimshian have four moieties (which they call *phratries*): Wolf, Eagle, Raven/Frog, and Killerwhale/Bear/Fireweed. The Tlingit have two moieties, the Raven/Crow and the Eagle/Wolf—depending on the time period. The Haida also have two, the Eagle and Raven. All three peoples are matrilineal, meaning that legitimacy and moiety descend from the mother, and boys are trained by their uncles (their mother's brothers) rather than their fathers.

From time immemorial, a river's mouth was the prize site for a Native village because of the wealth of salmon, herring, and hooligan that congregate there annually, and the seals, whales, and birds that follow the fish. (Fish at river mouths are always in top shape; fish farther up the waterway cease eating in their spawning quest, and are less desirable.) Plank houses were laid out following the curve of the shoreline, usually with the chief's house in the center. Each house had a name, like Moon House, Beaver House, or House Where People Always Want to Go. If the owner was rich enough to commission a frontal totem, this pole was erected between the house and the shore, facing approaching canoes.

Chiefs bore both traditional and personal names. Traditional names included Sigai ("the open sea") or Nankilstlas ("he whose voice is obeyed"). A traditional name was handed down with the office. The chief of the Wrangell area bore the traditional name of Shakes or Se.ks (the dot indicates a sound for which English has no equivalent).

Northwest Coast peoples lived in relative isolation, although there were occasional intertribal raids. Peace was the norm, however, and neighbors kept in touch with each other through trade in goods transported in their impressive seagoing canoes. Iridescent abalone came from as far away as Monterey Bay. Other goods—some from inland populations—included elk hides, moose skins, copper, mountain-goat wool, and ornamental shells. Trade was so important that trading partners often married into each other's family.

Trade was central to amassing wealth. With wealth, a chief could prove his social status by holding a feast called a potlatch. The potlatch, or "giving," is a formal distribution of goods that reasserts claims to property and privilege. At these events, which could go on for five days or more, chiefs distributed everything from coppers (shield-shaped copper objects) to furs to carved oil dishes. Anthropologist H. G. Barnett wrote in 1938, "Virtue rests in publicly disposing of wealth, not in its mere acquisition and accumulation."

Most missionaries and some early anthropologists saw no virtue in these huge giveaways. They saw them as economic suicide, "pagan" or "megalomaniacal."

As new trade goods came into the country with the arrival of Europeans and Americans, potlatch gifts began to include button blankets, Hudson's Bay blankets, samovars, treadle sewing machines, gramophones, sacks of flour, and pool tables. Elaborate oratory was employed to welcome invited guests, narrate tribal history, and pay compliments to the chief. Family heirlooms bearing clan crests would be paraded, and songs, dancing, and feasting were all part of the festivities. Every potlatch required such an abundance of food that leftovers would be carried away. Typical potlatch dishes were smoked salmon, dried fish, berries mixed with hooligan oil, and oil and wild crab apples mixed with snow.

The cultures of all three groups included potlatches—events expected of clans or high-ranking figures. Potlatch occasions included weddings, naming a child, or erecting a totem pole. Haida parents might hold a potlatch to establish the position of a young boy as heir presumptive. The Tlingit potlatch was often a series of rituals to mourn the death of a chief. The first served to reward the opposite moiety for conducting the funeral rites. The second introduced the new chief. The third celebrated the building of the new chief's house. The fourth might raise a mortuary pole in memory of the deceased chief.

How long has all this been going on? Pacific Northwest peoples have lived along this coast for 7,000 to 10,000 years. One site at Blue Jacket Creek on Masset Inlet has yielded evidence 3,500 years old of woodworking tools such as wedges, hammers, adzes, and chisel blades.

The Tsimshian are distinguished from the Haida and Tlingit in two important ways. First, their language seems to have no relationship to any other language, in either North America or Asia. Second, the Tsimshian did not settle in Southeast Alaska until historic times. This people originally lived along the Nass and Skeena rivers in British Columbia. In the 1830s some relocated to the Hudson's Bay Company trading post at Port Simpson. In 1857 a young Anglican missionary, William Duncan, came to educate the Tsimshian. In 1862, to separate his flock from liquor and other unhealthy influences, Duncan led a party of 50 back to their original lands and established a model village called Metlakatla. In 1881 Duncan had a falling out with his church leaders. The U.S. government

A HARMONIOUS PATTERN

The coast-line of Alaska is about twenty-six thousand miles long, more than twice as long as all the rest of the United States. The islands of the Alexander Archipelago, with the straits, channels, canals, sounds, passages, and fiords, form an intricate web of land and water embroidery sixty or seventy miles wide, fringing the lofty icy chain of coast mountains from Puget Sound to Cook Inlet, and, with infinite variety, the general pattern is harmonious throughout its whole extent of nearly a thousand miles. Here you glide into a narrow channel hemmed in by mountain walls, forested down to the water's edge, where there is no distant view, and your attention is concentrated on the objects close about you—the crowded spires of the spruces and hemlocks rising higher and higher on the steep green slopes; stripes of paler green where winter avalanches have cleared away the trees, allowing grasses and willows to spring up; zigzags of cascades appearing and disappearing among the bushes and trees; short, steep glens with brawling streams hidden beneath alder and dogwood, seen only where they emerge on the brown algae of the shore; and retreating hollows, with lingering snow-banks marking the fountains of ancient glaciers. The steamer is often so near the shore that you may distinctly see the cones clustered on the tops of the trees, and the ferns and bushes at their feet.

–John Muir, describing the Inside Passage on his first trip to Alaska in 1879, *Travels in Alaska*, 1915

gave him permission to relocate his community on Annette Island, 18 miles from Ketchikan. Duncan and 825 Tsimshian relocated in 1887 and built New Metlakatla. The island is the only Indian reservation in Alaska.

THE EXPLORERS' IMPACT

In 1774 the Spaniard Juan Perez became the first European to trade with the Haida. In the forty years following 1787, the previously isolated Haida were visited by hundreds of European and American ships. Explorers included Captain James Cook, Captain George Vancouver, Lieutenant (later Commander)

Fringed ceremonial blankets such as this are worn by Tlingits to significant events such as funerals.

Nathaniel Portlock, George Dixon, John Meares, Captain Joseph Billings, Commander Edward Belcher, Hudson's Bay Co. executive Sir George Simpson, Alexander Baranof, navigator Andrei Khlebnikov, Nikolai Rezanov (one of the founders of the Russian-American Company), naval officer Iurii Fedorovich Lisiansky, French sea captain Etienne Marchand, naval officer/fur trader Camille de Roquefeuil, and Captain Robert Gray. Between 1787 and 1809 at least 64 American ships traded off the Northwest Coast.

These explorers brought blue cloth, blue beads, and iron to trade—but they also brought new diseases. In the late 1830s the first of a series of smallpox epidemics ravaged the Northwest Coast, carrying off about half the Haida by the close of the decade. In the mid-1850s Haida men began looking for work in Victoria and Nanaimo. Many villages were abandoned by 1900.

In prehistoric times villages were sometimes relocated following fires or to elude enemies bent on capturing slaves. But as European and American new-comers arrived, they sometimes appropriated the sites of villages and forced villagers to move away. Some relocated in the constant jockeying among chiefs for the best position relative to a trading post. Later reasons for moving included opportunities for schooling children, attending church, or working for cash. Traditional fish-camp sites were abandoned as tribal members instead labored at canneries during the summer.

NEW CLAIMS TO SOUTHEAST ALASKA

In the late 18th century, Russian interests attempted to move down the coast through Prince William Sound and into the Inside Passage, but they met with fierce Tlingit resistance and a challenge from the British. The chief manager of the Russian-American Company, Alexander Baranof, was anxious to establish a trading foothold in Southeast Alaska before another nation beat him to it. In 1794,

The start of something big: an early example of canned salmon.

Baranof dispatched a fleet of 500 one- to three-man *bidarkas* (Native kayaks) to Icy Bay and Yakutat Bay. The party's hunt was successful, bringing back 900 sea-otter skins. But they encountered the English ships *Discovery* and *Chatham*, and Captain George Vancouver contested their claim to the area.

Natalia Shelikov, head of the Northwestern American Company, grew concerned about the British protests. She wrote to the Russian empress, "Now is the time to settle the question as to the boundary line between the Russian possessions and the English as there is a danger that they might make us abandon them altogether." Settlements in Cook Inlet and Prince William Sound were at risk, as well as the potential south of Lituya Bay, a promising territory she described as "the places of our dreams and imagination."

Baranof was instructed to explore farther south and bury tablets claiming the territory. During the summer of 1795 he visited Chilkat and Sitka. Delayed by

This 1897 board game played off popular perceptions of the Klondike Gold Rush.

injuries, storms, and shipwrecks, Baranof was not ready to set up a permanent outpost at Sitka until four years later.

The Tlingit cleverly played the British against the Russians. In 1799 Baranof watched as traders from Britain and the United States bartered for 2,000 sea-otter furs. The Russians had little in the way of trade goods, while the Tlingit managed to trade for woolen cloth, handfuls of beads, and excellent muskets and pistols manufactured in Boston and London.

But Baranof believed he had laid a "strong foundation" for Russia's occupying southeast Alaska, and sailed back to Kodiak in April 1800. Two years later, on the morning of June 26, 1802, Tlingit warriors overwhelmed the Sitka fort, burning it and killing many Russians, Native hunters, and their families. The Russians,

TAKU GLACIER

ALASKA EXCURSIONS   STEAMSHIP "SPOKANE"

SEASON 1903

LUNCH

SOUP—CLAM BROTH

VEAL CUTLETS BREADED, TOMATO SAUCE

STEWED LAMB, PARISIENNE POTATOES

BAKED CHEESE ON TOAST   APPLE FRITTERS

COLD ROAST BEEF   ROAST CHICKEN   ROAST PORK

CORNED TONGUE   HAM

COSMOPOLITAN SALAD

RICE   CAULIFLOWER   BAKED, BOILED AND MASHED NEW POTATOES

GREEN APPLE PIE   MINCE PIE

CURRANT BUNS   ASSORTED PASTRY

STEWED APRICOTS   STEWED PEARS   STEWED PRUNES

PRESERVED PEACHES   ASSSORTED JAMS

ORANGE ICE   FRUITS IN SEASON

CHEESE—SWISS   EDAM   OREGON CREAM   ROQUEFORT   AMERICAN

TOASTED CRACKERS

TEA   COFFEE   CHOCOLATE   COCOA   MILK

WEDNESDAY, JULY 8TH

The early cruises were stylish too; this menu dates from 1903

under Baranof, fought back by retaking the fort in 1804. The Tlingit nation did not immediately give up. They destroyed the Russian settlement at Yakutat in August 1805, and attempted to destroy the fort at Konstantinovsk in Prince William Sound. But gradually the Sitka Tlingit made peace with the Russians, re-establishing trade by exchanging halibut for fishhooks.

Despite the distractions of the Civil War, President Abraham Lincoln and Secretary of State William Seward could not ignore Alaska. They sent my ancestor, Gustavus Vasa Fox, assistant secretary of the Navy, on a secret mission to Russia to negotiate for its purchase. Faced with a decimated sea-otter population and increased competition from British and American whalers and traders, Russia finally agreed to the sale for $7.2 million, or two cents per acre.

"Russian-Alaska" became part of the United States in 1867, and Seward believed the new territory would more than pay for itself in furs, walrus ivory, fish, jade, gold, and timber. The vast territory, classed as a "department," was placed under the control of the U.S. Army. For the next 15 years the military ruled by misrule. Despite the natural riches of the place, no one paid much attention except prospectors, missionaries, educators, and visiting scientists. Ernest Gruening, Alaska's governor in the 1940s and '50s, called it an "era of total neglect."

In 1911, 44 years and eight presidents after the Alaska Purchase, President Theodore Roosevelt realized the territory had population as well as resources and inquired into the needs of its indigenous inhabitants. He asked Navy lieutenant George Thornton Emmons to write a report. Emmons first described the Eskimos, Athabaskans, and Aleuts of the Arctic and Interior. Then he turned to the people of southeast Alaska and wrote:

"The Tlingit, Haidas, and Tsimsheans, who occupy the narrow continental shore and adjacent islands, number some 6,000 souls and live in comparative comfort under very favorable conditions in large, well-built villages along the coast and channel ways. Here the climate is mild and healthful, wood and water are on every hand, fish life is abundant, and game is more than sufficient for their wants. They are intelligent, honest, and good workers; an accumulative, thrifty people, quick to learn, and anxious to improve their condition." All they asked, wrote a sympathetic Emmons, who had lived among them, is to have what American citizens have: "educational advantages . . ., protection in their rights to hold property and to locate mineral lands, citizenship when qualified, and the establishment of hospitals at central points."

The Organic Act of 1884 had provided Alaska with a territorial governor and basic law enforcement, but not representation in Washington, D.C. The territory was mostly ignored, despite lobbying efforts by Judge James Wickersham and others. Alaska's first congressional delegate was finally appointed in 1906, and Juneau made capital three years later.

Teddy Roosevelt, convinced by Emmons's arguments, convened a territorial legislature in 1912. At that time the total population, Native and Caucasian, numbered about 70,000. Few improvements were made in taming the wilderness until the threat of World War II brought in military personnel, and bases were established at Anchorage, Whittier, Fairbanks, Nome, Sitka, Delta Junction, Kodiak, and Dutch Harbor islands in the Aleutians. Meanwhile, Alaskans continued to struggle to gain the right to govern themselves. Finally, on January 3, 1959, "The Last Frontier" became the 49th state.

The Lower 48 usually turns its attention to Alaska in regard to a few key topics: tourism, environmental protection laws, Native rights, and oil production. (Before the Sarah Palin vice presidency nomination, that is.) Oil is the state's greatest export, and most of it comes from Prudhoe Bay, the nation's largest oil field. In the '70s, the Alaska Pipeline was built to transport the oil to the southern, and ice-free, port of Valdez. While U.S. oil consumption has steadily increased, oil production in Prudhoe Bay has actually decreased (it peaked in the '80s) due to the limits of existing wells and the deterioration of the 800-mile-long pipeline.

The 1971 Alaska Native Claims Settlement Act changed the lives of Native Alaskans forever. The act compensated indigenous peoples for property historically occupied or used by non-Natives with $962.5 million and 44 million acres of land. Native populations organized into 13 regional corporations, each taking a portion of the settlement. As shareholders in the corporations, Native Alaskans have had to wrestle with the transition from subsistence living to managing modern companies, going from traplines to tuxedoes almost overnight. Construction, environmental services, and government work are among the major employers. One of these corporations is Sealaska, the largest private landowner in Southeast, with headquarters in Juneau. The next federal regulation to make as much a difference was the 1976 Molly Hooch Case, which granted local secondary education to every community.

Alaska is a place of superlatives and contradictions: more bald eagles than all the other states combined; the only capitol with no highway access; a population that grew 32.4 percent during the 1970s; and a holiday no other state celebrates— Alaska Day, the anniversary of the formal transfer of the territory and the raising of the U.S. flag at Sitka on Oct. 18, 1867. It's a place to experience, and one that will likely exceed your expectations in every way.

KETCHIKAN

Often the first port of call along Alaska's Inside Passage, Ketchikan rolls out a scenic welcome mat to coastal rain forest and the hardy folk who call it home. Even before you reach town, the sight of deer or bears swimming across Wrangell Narrows will let you know you're not in Kansas anymore. You'll know, as photographer Ansel Adams put it, you're "closer to elemental things."

Like Juneau, Ketchikan is sandwiched between a hard place, Deer Mountain, and a wet channel, Tongass Narrows. The town perches on the southwest side of a larger island, Revillagigedo—often shortened to Revilla. A smaller island, Gravina, lies just offshore and is the site of Ketchikan airport, linked to town by ferry. The town proper meanders like a silk scarf for six miles along the available strip of coast, with wooden stairways standing in for streets where slopes rise steeply.

Like most Inside Passage destinations, Ketchikan is surrounded by Tongass National Forest. As if that weren't bounty enough, Ketchikan is only about 30 miles west of the 2.2 million-acre wilderness of Misty Fiords National Monument.

How to access these oases? Take a leaf from the locals, who board floatplanes and charter vessels as casually as residents of the Big Apple or D.C. hail a cab or swing aboard the metro. Floatplanes and charter boats can speed you to destinations such as Misty Fiords or Prince of Wales Island (20 miles west of town), known for its caves.

Ketchikan uneasily wears the title "rain capital of Alaska," bestowed in recognition of its average annual precipitation: 160 inches. The 15,000 friendly residents take fog and damp in stride, wearing knee-high rubber boots everywhere, even to the theater, and staging slug races during the Blueberry Arts Festival. They practically purr as they take deep breaths of some of North America's freshest air—washed clean by frequent deluges of "liquid sunshine."

KETCHIKAN THEN

Humans have found this area habitable for at least 10,000 years. In July 1996 paleontologists investigating On Your Knees Cave on northern Prince of Wales Island discovered the partial skeleton of a man whose remains were dated at more than 10,000 years old. Ongoing digs are rewriting archaeological theories about the peopling of America.

Genteel-looking Creek Street was once the red-light district's main drag.

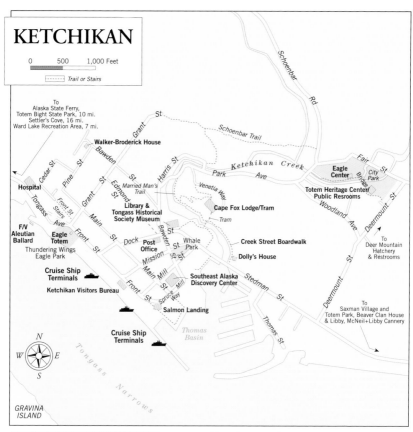

KETCHIKAN

0   500   1,000 Feet

········· Trail or Stairs

To
Alaska State Ferry,
Totem Bight State Park, 10 mi.
Settler's Cove, 16 mi.
Ward Lake Recreation Area, 7 mi.

Schoenbar Rd

Grant St

Schoenbar Trail

Walker-Broderick House

Bawden

Cedar St

Pine

Grant St

Edmond St

Harris St

Ketchikan Creek

Park Ave

Eagle Center

Fair St

City Park

Bridge

Hospital

Married Man's Trail

Venetia Way

Totem Heritage Center/ Public Resrooms

Tongass

Front St

Stairs

Ave

Main St

Married Man's Trail

Library &
Tongass Historical
Society Museum

Cape Fox Lodge/Tram

Tram

Woodland Ave

Deermount St

F/V
Aleutian
Ballard

Eagle
Totem

Front St

Dock St

Post
Office

Bawden St

Whale
Park

Creek Street Boardwalk

To
Deer Mountain
Hatchery
& Restrooms

Thundering Wings
Eagle Park

Mission St

St

Dolly's House

Cruise Ship
Terminals

Main St

Mill St

Southeast Alaska
Discovery Center

Stedman St

Deermount St

Ketchikan Visitors Bureau

Front St

Spruce Way

Salmon Landing

To
Saxman Village and
Totem Park, Beaver Clan House
& Libby, McNeil+Libby Cannery

N

W   E

S

Cruise Ship
Terminals

Thomas
Basin

Thomas St

Tongass   Narrows

GRAVINA
ISLAND

Slices of Ketchikan life.

FAQs

What does the town's name mean?
It's most likely derived from a traditional Tlingit term, *Kitchik-him,* which has etymological associations with rivers and thundering eagle wings. However, a 1924 volume tracing the early explorer George Vancouver's journeys says the name means "wedged," a reference to Gravina Island, which appears wedged against the larger Revilla Island. Local historians assert that *Kitschkhin* translates as "Kitschk's stream," after a Tlingit fisherman from Cape Fox or Tongass who established a seasonal camp near Ketchikan Creek in prehistoric times.

Do people live here year-round?
Yes. Or, as Dave Kiffer, director of Historic Ketchikan Inc., puts it: "There are wetter places on earth, but hardly anyone chooses to live there."

Where is the Tongass?
Everywhere—that is, any spot that is neither private property nor Native corporation land. The Tongass National Forest encompasses most of the land in the Inside Passage, 17 million acres.

What do you call baby salmon?
When they hatch from fertilized eggs, they are "fry." When they begin feeding, call them "fingerlings"—but don't call them late to dinner. When they reach four to eight inches, they become "smolts."

Ketchikan's waterfront in the early 20th century.

As elsewhere in the Inside Passage, place names around Ketchikan hold history like brimming cups. "Saxman," for example, refers to Samuel Saxman, an American teacher lost with two other men during the winter of 1886 while seeking a new village site. "Revillagigedo" refers to the Spanish explorers seeking new territory along this rugged coast. Spain sent three separate expeditions (1774, 1775, and 1779, the third led by Juan Francisco de la Bodega y Quadra). Bodega y Quadra named Revillagigedo for the Count of Revilla Gigedo, viceroy of Mexico in the late 1700s.

British captain George Vancouver lavishly applied names, including changing Canal de Nuestra Senora del Carmen to Clarence Strait to honor the Duke of Clarence. One afternoon in August 1793, Vancouver was sailing in the Clarence Strait when a party of Stikine Tlingit approached his vessels from the western shore. An inferior chief, Kanaut, was allowed to board Vancouver's ship and offered to introduce the captain to the region's most powerful chief, Ononnistoy. On August 31, Ononnistoy presented himself, and was dazzled with fireworks, bread, molasses, rum, and wine.

Spanish explorers failed to establish a permanent settlement in Stikine territory. That task was accomplished by an Irishman, Mike Martin of Portland, Oregon,

THE HAIDA WORLD

To the Haida the world was like the edge of a knife cutting between the depths of the sea, which to them symbolized the underworld, and the forested mountainside, which marked the transition to the upper world . . . . On the one side they faced treacherous ocean currents; on the other, dense forests.

Perhaps because of their precarious position, they embellished the narrow human zone of their villages with a profusion of boldly carved monuments and brightly painted emblems signifying their identity. Throughout their villages these representations of the creatures of the upper and lower worlds presented a balanced statement of the forces of their universe. Animals and birds represented the upper world of the forest and the heavens, while sea mammals, especially killer whales, and fishes symbolized the underworld. The transition between realms was bridged by such amphibians as frogs, beavers, and otters. Hybrid mythological creatures, such as sea grizzlies and sea wolves, symbolized a merging of cosmic zones.

—George F. MacDonald, *Chiefs of the Sea and Sky,* 1989

who was determined to capitalize on the area's fisheries. A saltery had been erected at the mouth of Fish Creek in 1883, and the first salmon cannery opened in 1886. Martin came to the area in 1885 and acquired 160 acres from Chief Kyan. In 1888 Martin obtained 640 acres of land from a Haida named Paper Nose Charlie, built a cannery, and filed incorporation papers in 1900. (Another version of the story says that Charlie was a Kwakiutl Indian, and that he wore a paper nose after a Wrangell Tlingit bit off his real nose in a violent altercation.)

The Inside Passage experienced several gold rushes in the early 1900s, and the new town became a miners' supply center. Salmon canning continued to flourish. In 1924 Ketchikan canned 125,000 cases of salmon, and in the 1930s there were more than a dozen canneries in operation. So much salmon was harvested here that Ketchikan was crowned "salmon capital of the world" and briefly became Alaska's largest city. But overfishing took its toll, hastened by mismanagement by the Fish and Wildlife Service of the Department of the Interior. The salmon canning industry began to wane in the 1940s.

Local traffic: seaplanes and cruise ships in the Tongass Narrows.

During World War II, logging and pulping stepped up as the main sources of income. Western hemlock was harvested for shipping containers, furniture, railroad ties, and mining timbers. Yellow cedar, with its even grain, was harvested for flooring, doors, sashes, and cabinets. By 1949 Ketchikan had a large sawmill and a box factory. In 1953 the Ward Cove pulp mill opened northwest of town, processing spruce and hemlock for the production of rayon and cellophane. For decades the mill was the biggest employer in southeast Alaska.

KETCHIKAN NOW *map page 32*

Today debates simmer between those who wish to clear-cut timber and those who want to preserve old-growth forest. Bumper stickers mark the turf of "tree-huggers" and tree fellers, while global warming puts a new spin on the future of logging the Tongass. Meanwhile, Ketchikan depends on fishing and tourism. The latter developed after Pan American Airlines started flying between Seattle and Ketchikan in 1940. Now you can fly to Ketchikan from Seattle in just 90 minutes, making it accessible to the Lower 48 in less time, and at a lower cost, than any other part of Alaska.

Mariculture has a slippery toehold on the local economy. When the Ketchikan Pulp Company closed its mill in 1997, community leaders promoted a floating upwelling system (FLUPSY) to encourage shellfish farming. The system helps reduce oyster spat mortality and can halve the time needed to cultivate an oyster crop. Today there are oyster and little neck clam farms near Prince of Wales Island, and geoduck farms near Ketchikan and Etolin Island (off Wrangell).

Ketchikan describes itself as "three miles long and three blocks wide," an indication of how it skirts the sinuous waterfront from the ferry terminal to Thomas Basin and beyond. In summer Ketchikan bustles much like Juneau and other Inside Passage towns: floatplanes take off and touch down, fishing boats offload at canneries as gulls scream for scraps, and ferries and cruise ships offload excited visitors. No matter the weather, residents carry on, picnicking, dipnet fishing, and playing baseball in the rain.

WALKING TOUR

Begin at the "Welcome to Alaska's First City" sign near the cruise-ship docks. A walking-tour map is available at the nearby Ketchikan Visitors Bureau (131 Front St.; 907/225–6166; www.visit-ketchikan.com). Stroll along Mission Street to **Whale Park** to see the Chief Kyan Totem. At the far end of the park

KID STUFF

- Let the kids run around the two dozen tall and small totems at **Saxman Village** (907/225–4846). At the park's Edmund C. DeWitt Carving Center, you can peer through the open window to watch Native artists carve a totem, canoe, or paddle—and you may even be fortunate enough to have a carver invite you inside.

- Get an eyeful of top timber athletes at the **Great Alaskan Lumberjack Show** (Spruce Mill Way; 907/225–9050). They demonstrate speed climbing, axe throwing, and carving with chain saws, plus the almost comedic balancing act of log rolling. There are 3 to 5 performances daily, May through September, each lasting 90 minutes, and they take place in a heated, covered grandstand.

- Head for **Creek Street** and Married Man's Trail to see spawning salmon climbing the fish ladder up the falls. The bridge offers a good view. Kings spawn from the end of July through August; coho spawn from Thanksgiving through Christmas.

is the Kadjuk or Chief Johnson Totem, a replica of a 1901 original. (Kadjuk is a mythical bird based on the golden eagle.) Turn left to reach the 28-foot Raven Stealing the Sun Totem and the **Tongass Historical Museum** (629 Dock St.; 907/225–5600), which shares a building with the town library. Museum displays range from stone tools to contemporary art, giving insights into the Tlingit, Tsimshian, and Haida cultures. Summer exhibits highlight "everything we can possibly stuff in" about local history.

Turn back toward Whale Park to reach the bridge across Ketchikan Creek. (Look for a sculpture standing in the water paying tribute to salmon.) Cross the bridge to **Creek Street.** This wooden thoroughfare, built on pilings around 1900, was the main drag of a flourishing red-light district until the early 1950s. The district was reached by the so-called Married Man's Trail from Park Avenue. During Prohibition some of the bawdy houses became speakeasies, with liquor from Outside rowed in on high tides. Many of Creek Street's 20 houses have been restored to suit more genteel businesses like the marvelously cluttered **Parnassus Books** (5 Creek St.; 907/225–7690). Get a hint of Prohibition-era naughtiness at

Dolly's House Museum (24 Creek St.; 907/225–6329), a former brothel that exhibits garters, hats, and the sewing machine of Big Dolly Arthur, a madam and "working girl" into the 1950s. Dolly charged $3; a tour costs more ($5).

For a view over downtown to the Tongass Narrows, turn back toward the bridge and board the **funicular** ($2) that climbs to the **West Coast Cape Fox Lodge** (800 Venetia Way; 907/225–8001). The 1990 hotel's lobby and staircase are decorated with beautifully carved panels in the Tlingit formline tradition. Exit on Venetia Avenue to see the circle of modern totems, "The Council of the Clans."

Continue along Venetia to Park Avenue. Turn right on Park, and follow it to City Park and the **Deer Mountain Tribal Hatchery and Eagle Center** (1158 Salmon Rd.; 800/225–5158). Here you can see king and coho fingerlings, rainbow trout and steelhead, and photograph eagles up close. There is a narrated tour. Cross over a pedestrian bridge to **Totem Heritage Cultural Center** (601 Deermount St.; 907/225–5900). The rare birds here are more than 30 unrestored (but preserved) totem poles, some nearly two centuries old, plus fragments of others retrieved from deserted Tlingit and Haida vil-

Two of Ketchikan's striking totems: Chief Kyan (left, ca. 1900) and Chief Johnson (right).

lages. The center hosts classes in beading, basketry, carving, and silver engraving.

This walking tour, mostly on level ground, requires three to four hours. If you're in town during a July weekend, consider spending an evening watching a performance of the *Fish Pirate's Daughter* (Ted Ferry Civic Center, 800 Venetia Way; 907/225–4792), by the First City Players. This melodrama by locals Bill Kinerk and Jim Alguire, based on Ketchikan's history, has been running since 1965.

BRIEF EXCURSIONS

Walk to the corner of Main and Pine streets to view the **Chief Kyan Totem.** Legend has it that touching the pole guarantees money within 24 hours, so now's the time to buy that lottery ticket. There are some noteworthy early-20th-century buildings near this intersection too. Check out the turreted **Monrean House** (500 Main St.), a 1904 Queen Anne-style residence. Two blocks away at 541 Pine Street stands the Craftsman-style **Walker-Broderick House** (c. 1916).

Rent a kayak and launch at Bar Point Basin marina. Paddle into Thomas Basin and then up Ketchikan Creek at high water. The trip requires two to three hours. **Southeast Sea Kayaks** (1621 Tongass Ave., 907/225–1258) offers rentals and guided trips; beginners receive instruction.

Listen to the clip-clop of four draft horses as they pull you along in an open-sided trolley on an easygoing excursion run by **Seahorse Ventures** (2878 S. Tongass Ave.; 907/225–5713). A guide accompanied by a gorgeous husky sup-

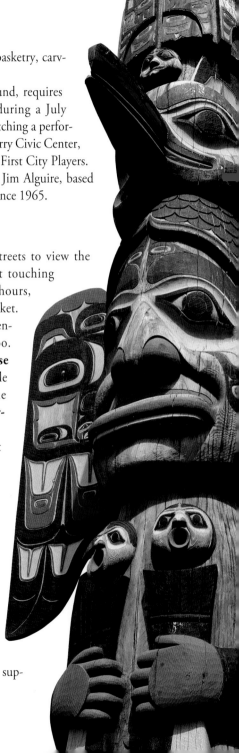

MISTY FIORDS

Nearly as large as Glacier Bay National Park but not as well known, Misty Fiords National Monument offers a whopping 2.2 million acres of breathtaking wilderness playing hide-and-seek in the shifting mist. Some of the protected land covers the east coast of Revillagigedo Island, while the rest lies on the mainland between the Behm and Portland canals. Shaped by glaciers and annually drenched by 150 inches of snow and rain, this land was set aside as protected territory in 1978. Steep cliffs rise as much as 3,000 feet above the ocean.

Although the Inside Passage is less seismic than the Aleutian Chain, it occasionally experiences earthquakes and once had active volcanoes. If you're interested in seeing evidence of Alaska's steamy history, consider a 3½-hour catamaran trip that includes New Eddystone Rock, a giant chunk of basalt known as a volcanic core. The rock juts out of the water in the middle of Behm Canal.

Like Glacier Bay National Park, Misty Fiords is so large that you may prefer to view it from the air. Or you could rent a Forest Service cabin; some have ocean moorings while others, set on alpine lakes, are equipped with their own small boats. Whatever your taste, the monument is superb from any angle. The Ketchikan-Misty Fiords Ranger District is the best source of info on boating and camping in "Misty" (907/225–2148; www.fs.fed.us/r10/tongass).

Hopping a floatplane in the Misty Fiords.

plies in-depth narration during this 45-minute jaunt, with photo stops at strategic points. Learn the history of the port, visit a Klondike-era park with original fountain and ponds, see the totem at Whale Park, a 100-foot mural painted by Tlingit kids, and a plank street still in use.

Head into the woods with an **Adventure Kart Expedition** (Cape Fox Tours, 907/225–4846; www.capefoxtours.com). A jet boat whisks you to a privately-owned site in the White River/George Inlet area, where you can splash through mud puddles on an 8-horsepower dune buggy engineered especially for backcountry use. Drivers must be licensed, but youngsters may ride as passengers. Deer, ravens, and eagles can be spotted on this trip. Return to town by bus, or take a bus out and boat back.

How about a **guided fly-fishing tour** to White River to fish for steelhead and silver and pink salmon? **Cape Fox Tours** (907/225–4846; www.capefoxtours. com) runs a trip that takes care of the 45-minute van ride each way, with three hours of fishing; waders and gear are provided. More than half the guides are Tlingit or Haida, and happy to chat about their traditional way of life.

Ketchikan has a vibrant art scene. Take some time to visit its **art galleries** and, if the timing is right, events like the Blueberry Arts Festival in August and the Winter Arts Faire on the weekend after Thanksgiving. Both provide excellent opportunities to purchase local arts and crafts, everything from art-paper mood lamps to bluegrass CDs.

To sample Ketchikan's taste in witty public art, take a gander at the "Pyling Cap" series by Terry Pyles. Inspired by art in Barcelona, Pyles created these mosaic tile toppers for the 18-inch dock pilings in 2006. One shows an auger snail, a second is the common snail, and the third is a flock of goose barnacles. Look for them near **Pyles' Dockside Gallery** (5 Salmon Landing; 907/225–2858).

LONGER OUTINGS

Take the **Best of Ketchikan Land & Sea Tour** (Cape Fox Tours, 907/225–4846) to George Inlet. This narrated 3½-hour tour carries you through the Tongass Narrows to the Libby, McNeill, and Libby Cannery (1913–1958). In addition to learning about cannery history, seine fishing, and fish traps, you'll go to Saxman Village, where you are introduced to both carvers and totems, and given time to shop and take photos. Transportation is by jet boat and bus.

If the totems at the Totem Heritage Cultural Center have only sparked your appetite, there are dozens more waiting. Start your engines at the **Southeast**

EARLY INSIDE PASSAGE CRUISES

Sightseers came to the Inside Passage hard on the heels of the map-makers and missionaries who spread word of its magnificent vistas. By the 1880s visitors were regularly taking the Pacific Coast Steamship Company's vessels north from San Francisco or Portland. By 1886 these trips were so popular that the steamship company doubled its summer sailings.

Many of the earliest passengers penned enthusiastic, detailed books or articles that defrosted the notion of "Seward's ice box" and drummed up tourism. Eliza Scidmore, correspondent for the *St. Louis Globe Democrat* and the *New York Times*, compiled her *Journeys to Alaska* after an 1883 paddlewheeler cruise. She reported on the trade in shining bracelets pounded from silver dollars, spoons steamed from mountain goat horn, and intricate baskets.

By the end of the 1800s Native artists were responding to the tourist influx by producing items that could be transported easily, such as totem poles less than a yard high, baskets in the shape of tea kettles, jewelry, and tiny spoons pounded from silver dollars. Since tourists were slow to appreciate Native art, traditional works were often demeaned as grotesque curios. A 1912 Alaska Steamship Company brochure promised tourists "crude gropings toward art by a primitive people."

Souvenirs were an attraction, but so were glaciers. The panorama began at Wrangell, with the Stickeen Glacier on the nearby eponymous river. Then, as ships steamed toward Skagway they passed a dazzling parade of icy giants: Patterson, Bairds, Young, Yosemite, Toyatt, Windom, Taku, Eagle, Auk, Meade, and Dewey. Glacier Bay was ringed with the Muir, Pacific, Hugh Miller, and Geikie glaciers. These were set off by smaller glaciers and dramatic waterfalls too numerous to name.

World War I put a crimp in cruising, but the industry quickly revived. The Inside Passage route was endlessly praised. A 1930 brochure of the Pacific Steamship Company gushed, "For over one thousand miles the World's Smoothest Waterway unwinds its silver screen of scenic wonderland, each immense foot of celluloid disclosing a gem of ocean and mountain beauty more thrilling than the one just rolled into the background of our memory." (A 9- to 12-day cruise of 2,350 miles cost $100, with meals.)

Cruise-ship traffic continues to grow. In 1990, about 250,000 visitors arrived in Ketchikan by cruise ship; in 2007, about 840,000 arrived. In 2007 Juneau received more than 900,000 cruise-ship visitors; if 5 ships tie up, that translates to 13,000 new faces in a single day.

Scooting out of town in sea kayaks.

Alaska Discovery Center (50 Main St.; 907/228–6214), where you can see contemporary totem poles and a realistic, life-size fish camp diorama.

Crave more? Drive, bike, or hike south 2½ miles on the Tongass Highway to ★Saxman Village Totem Park (907/225–4846). The two dozen totems at this site were brought here in the 1930s from abandoned villages on Tongass, Cat, Pennock, and Village islands, and from Kirk Point. They were arranged into a formal park with the aid of the Civilian Conservation Corps. The totems include the Bear-Kats Pole (based on the legend of a bear who fell in love with a hunter), the Wolf Pole, the Rock Oyster Pole, Loon Tree, and Three Eagles. The Beaver Clan House has interior house posts, but you must be on a Cape Fox Tour to enter. The two most photographed poles are the Abraham Lincoln Pole, which may refer to the U.S. revenue cutter *Lincoln*, and the William Seward, memorializing Seward's visit to the area in 1868, the year after the Alaska Purchase.

For dessert, drive nine miles north on the Tongass Highway to the 13-acre ★Totem Bight State Historical Park (907/247–8574). Flickers, the only woodpeckers to dine on the ground, may dart about as you take the short woodland

The clan house at Totem Bight State Historical Park.

trail through hemlocks to this lovely spot. The replica community house gives a real sense of dim, cedar-scented Tlingit interiors. Some of the park's 15 Haida and Tlingit totems are topped with the watchman figure, a lookout typically wearing a woven spruce-root hat.

If you've seen the Discovery Channel's *Deadliest Catch* program, you're familiar with the **F/V** *Aleutian Ballad.* Now you can get a firsthand taste of fishing from the deck of this crabbing vessel with the **Bering Sea Crab Fishermens' Tour** (Berth 3, Tender Float; 360/642–4935). Skilled fishermen share their daily life and stories from the sea. This is the real thing, but visitors are sheltered from the elements in an onboard heated amphitheater. Creatures brought to the surface are placed in a live tank for close inspection—before being released back into the Pacific.

Soak up incredible scenery in ★**Misty Fiords National Monument.** You can reach the park via a 30-mile floatplane or boat ride from Ketchikan. (Allow several hours for a flightseeing trip and at least a full day for a boat tour.) You'll have a good shot at spotting wildlife, as Misty Fiords is a haven for brown and black bears, Sitka deer, mink, river otters, and the occasional moose. The waters of Behm Canal teem with humpbacks, orcas, porpoises, sea lions, and seals.

For a seal's eye view, rent a kayak from Southeast Exposure (37 Potter Rd.; 907/225–8829) or sign up for a five-hour guided trip with Southeast Sea Kayaks (1621 Tongass Ave.; 907/225–1258). Twenty-foot tides make beach camping unsafe, but Forest Service cabins can be reserved. Alaska Travel Adventures (800/228–1905) is one of the best-known boat and flightseeing operators. *See* the "Misty Fiords" sidebar for more information.

To experience the atmosphere of a village with no road access, board a plane or ferry for the 12-mile journey to **Metlakatla** on Annette Island, the state's only Native reservation. The island was once a refuge for Canadians led by missionary William Duncan, but in 1891 Congress turned it over to the Tsimshian themselves. Now the town feels like a quiet pioneer settlement. About 1,600 people live here during the off-season, with the population jumping to 2,100 during fishing/tourist season. Activities include a 2½- to 4-hour bus tour of the community and the Duncan Cottage Museum (1891), a dance performance, and artist demonstrations. To book, call Metlakatla Tours (907/886–8687). Total excursion is 6 to 12 hours.

Try spelunking in one of the deepest caves in the United States. About 850 square miles of limestone lie beneath the Tongass National Forest. As water seeps into the limestone, it erodes sink holes, fissures, and cave systems to form a "karst landscape." Board the ferry to Hollis on Prince of Wales Island, then drive three hours to access the **El Capitan Underground Cave Tour.** El Capitan is Alaska's largest surveyed cave, with 12,000 feet of mapped passageways. The real treasure here is not the dizzying limestone and marble formations, but bones of bears, river otters, and other mammals, some dating back 12,000 years. Access is rated difficult, with plenty of uneven footing. Reserve a Forest Service guide two days in advance (907/828–3304). Free tours are offered Thursday through Saturday in summer; no children under age seven.

FAVORITE PLACES TO SHOP

One of the best places to browse is the **Saxman Village Store** (2711 Killerwhale Ave., 907/225–4421), which sells locally made totems, masks, carvings, and button blankets (ceremonial or "dancing" blankets decorated with mother-of-pearl buttons and totemic felt cutouts). Two blocks away is the **Saxman Arts Co-op** (907/225–1640), with similar offerings. Ask about old buttons in fish shapes, recycled from regalia long gone.

Hit the **Soho Coho Gallery** (5 Creek St.; 907/225–5954) to giggle over Ray Troll's zany T-shirts, lively books, limited edition serigraphs and "fish juju." Ray's personal slogan is "better living through difficult art." His refrigerator magnets swim in schools in supermarkets all over southeast Alaska. And he has netted talented friends, including illustrator Evon Zerbetz.

If you prefer malls, head for **Spruce Mill Mall** and **Salmon Landing Market** near the cruise-ship docks. Clothing, quilt fabric, silver jewelry, beads, and knickknacks are on display with local linocuts, art photography, and block prints.

For investment-level purchases, it's on to **Alaska Eagle Arts** (5 Creek St.; 907/225–8365) to see work by contemporary Quinault/Isleta-Pueblo artist Marvin Oliver. Internationally known, Oliver is a sculptor, mixed-media artist, and printmaker producing collectibles ranging from $3 note cards to Pendleton blanket designs and $100,000 bronzes.

For carvings in wood, jewelry, screen prints, and metal engravings, drop by **Ketchikan's Carver** (28 Creek St.; 907/225–3018). Ketchikan-born Tlingit artist Norman G. Jackson is a recognized master. Other carvers to reckon with include Bill Holm, Nathan Jackson (also of Ketchikan), Dwayne Pascol, and Wayne Price.

FAVORITE PLACES TO EAT

Alaska Fish House. Nibble on samples of alder-smoked salmon while pondering what to overnight to friends back home. In a neat silver building, Alaska Fish House is a year-round, cannery-style market for salmon, Dungeness crab, spot prawns, and other pristine goodies caught and flash-frozen by one painstaking fisherman, daily. From April through October, owners Chuck and Debby Slagle dish up tasty takeout: alder-grilled salmon, halibut and chips, and two-king chowder. The chowder is a steaming dream: smoked salmon, roasted salmon, roasted corn, thyme, and cream. The dining room recreates a 1940s state room. Dining on-site is by reservation only. *3 Salmon Landing, end of Main St.; 907/225–4055.* **$–$$**

WestCoast Cape Fox Lodge. This luxurious 72-room lodge, loaded with wood and stone accents, contains one of only three restaurants in Alaska reached by tram. Hotel guests and locals ride free; others pay $2. Specialties include halibut Olympia (baked with Bermuda onions) and seafood chowder. Servings are generous. Cape Fox serves oysters from Prince of Wales' aquatic farms. *800 Venetia Ave.; 907/225–8001.* **$$–$$$**

Alaskan Chef's Table. For something truly indulgent, consider a five-course seafood tasting menu served in a private dining room overlooking the harbor. Entertainment includes stories of Norwegian grandmothers in the basement of the Lutheran church, competing to cook Ketchikan's best fish cakes. There are also tales of stormy nights at sea. Your personal chef serves 10 dishes highlighting Alaska's sustainable wild seafood. The dinner includes hot- and cold-smoked salmon, saffron-infused bouillabaisse, halibut and king salmon, finished off with cappuccino brownies and rhubarb-blueberry bread pudding. *3 Salmon Landing; 907/617–4213.* **$$**

Ketchikan Coffee Company. This year-round lunch and coffee place opened in summer 2007, banning fried foods in favor of healthier options like grilled panini. You can still indulge your sweet tooth, though, with scones, cheesecake, and muffins. Rub shoulders with borough members who hold meetings here, brushing buttery crumbs off their notes. Live bluegrass and jazz bands play most Friday nights. *211 Stedman St.; 907/247–2326.* **$–$$**

WRANGELL

Like Sitka, Wrangell has witnessed several eras in its past—eras of Russian exploration, British fur trading, Russian occupation, economic boom accompanying gold rushes, and American logging and fishing. Like Juneau, much of its downtown rests on rock fill. And as at Treadwell, fierce fires in 1906 and 1952 gutted its historic core.

Wrangell is compact enough to tour on foot in a day. The inner harbor curves its protective arms around Chief Shakes Island. In summer the air thrums with the perfume and engine sounds of shrimp- and salmon-processing. Wrangell's history is closely tied to that of the Stikine River seven miles north. The Stikine is North America's fastest navigable river; from a prehistoric Tlingit trade route, it became the supply corridor for the 19th-century Stikine and Cassiar gold rushes. In 1897 and 1898 it earned fame as a water route to interior Canada during the Klondike gold rush. Wooded hillsides backed by snow-capped mountains form a striking backdrop—old hat to residents, but thrilling for *cheechakos* (newcomers) as their vessels approach the dock jutting out into Zimovia Strait.

WRANGELL THEN

During the thousands of years after early humans crossed the Bering land bridge, bands of hunters across the Arctic and Subarctic regions of Alaska migrated south seeking to expand their hunting territory. Avoiding the land's great swaths of ice, they traveled by watercraft, floating down the great rivers to the coast. Roughly 8,000 years ago, one adventurous Tlingit group in British Columbia descended the swift, 330-mile Stikine River. Soon their way was blocked by a great glacier—too rough to cross and too wide to circumvent. The cold, swirling river disappeared into a big hole. But where did the hole lead?

An elder volunteered to paddle his canoe into the frightening opening. "I will send a smoke signal if I come out safely," the man promised. He daringly aimed his craft at the gaping maw of the ice cave and was instantly out of sight. The people waited anxiously. Then the signal came. He was safe! The rest of the band followed the elder's lead, settling seven miles from the Stikine River delta, just south of modern Wrangell. The settlement was called Kots-lit-na (or Kotzlitzna) and the immigrant Tlingits became known as the Stikines (*stick-eens*).

The Eagle Totem guards the Tribal House of the Bear.

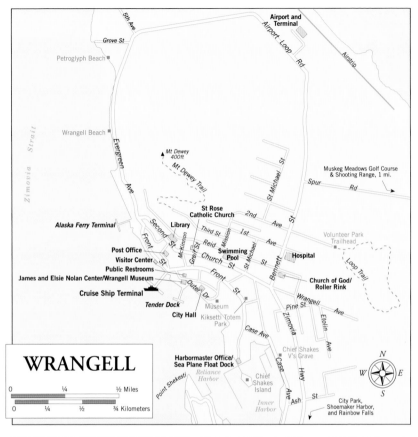

WRANGELL

0 ¼ ½ Miles

0 ¼ ½ ¾ Kilometers

Airport and Terminal

5th Ave

Grove St

Petroglyph Beach

Airport Loop Rd

Airstrip

Zimovia Strait

Wrangell Beach

Evergreen Ave

Mt Dewey 400ft

Mt Dewey Trail

St Michael St

Muskeg Meadows Golf Course & Shooting Range, 1 mi.

Spur Rd

St Rose Catholic Church

2nd Ave

St Michael St

Alaska Ferry Terminal

Library

Third St

1st Ave

Volunteer Park Trailhead

Second St

Mission St

Reid

Front St

McKinnon

Grief St

Church St

Swimming Pool

St Michael St

Bennett St

Hospital

Loop Trail

Post Office

Visitor Center

Public Restrooms

James and Elsie Nolan Center/Wrangell Museum

Cruise Ship Terminal

Outer Dr

Front St

Church of God/ Roller Rink

Wrangell Ave

Etolin Ave

Tender Dock

City Hall

Museum

Pine St

Zimovia Hwy

Kiksetti Totem Park

Case Ave

Harbormaster Office/ Sea Plane Float Dock

Chief Shakes V's Grave

Point Shekesti

Reliance Harbor

Chief Shakes Island

Case St

Ash St

N
W E
S

City Park, Shoemaker Harbor, and Rainbow Falls

Inner Harbor

Wrangell's history has been shaped by glaciers and the Stikine River.

FAQs

What do Alaskans mean by "Outside"?
This term, often uttered with a curled lip, indicates "the Lower 48"—that is, the rest of the United States. Because the Alaska Territory was ignored for decades after the Alaska Purchase, residents harbored considerable scorn for other Americans, and particularly for authorities far away in Washington, D.C. Aspects of this attitude linger, as in the bumper sticker, "We don't care how they do it Outside."

Do you accept U.S. currency?
As much as you can spare.

What is a "humpie"?
A humpie is a pink salmon, the smallest of the five species of Pacific salmon. Males on spawning migration develop a marked hump behind their heads.

Visitors welcomed to Chief Shakes's home, ca. 1916.

As the glacier retreated, the Stikines used the river to trade with the Athabascans, exchanging goods such as fish oil and strings of dried clams for beaver and land-otter pelts. When the Russians arrived, they wanted control of the valuable Stikine trade. In 1833 emissaries of the Russian-American Company under Dionysius Fedorovich Zarembo began building Redoubt Saint Dionysius on what is now called Wrangell Island. (These rudimentary fortified outposts typically consisted of a trading post, a manager's house, and a barracks surrounded by a palisade of upright logs.) A scant six years later the discouraged Russians sold the outpost to the British, who renamed it Fort Stikine, and traded copper kettles, cloth, and Hudson's Bay Company blankets to the Stikine for furs. To keep an eye on things, the Stikine chief, one of in a line of seven who took the name Shakes, moved his residence from Kots-lit-na 13 miles south to a small island in Wrangell's harbor. The Tlingits did not favor the use of their traditional trade routes by Hudson's Bay personnel. However, Native resistance became nominal after their population was halved during smallpox epidemics in 1836 and 1840.

In 1868, a year after America's Alaska Purchase, the trading settlement became a U.S. Army outpost called Fort Wrangell, named for Baron Ferdinand von Wrangel, chief manager for the Russian-American Company in the 1830s. Thus Wrangell became the only city in Alaska to have been governed by four nations.

CHIEF TOYATTE SPEAKS

In the course of time a change came over the spirit of our dreams. We became aware of the fact that we were not the only beings in the shape of man that inhabited this earth. White men appeared before us on the surface of the great waters in large ships which we called canoes. Where they came from we knew not, but supposed that they dropped from the clouds. The ship's sails we took for wings, and concluded that, like the birds of the air, they could fly as well as swim. As time advanced, the white men who visited our country introduced among us every thing that is produced by nature and the arts of man. They also told us of a God, a superior being, who created all things, even us the Indians . . . and that all mankind were His children . . . . We are not the same people that we were a hundred years ago . . . .

. . . We have been told that the President of the United States has control over all the people, both whites and Indians. . . . He purchased this country from Russia, and in purchasing it he purchased us. We had no choice or say in change of masters. The change has been made and we are content. All we ask is justice.

. . . If you will all assist us in doing good and quit selling whisky, we will soon make Fort Wrangell a quiet place and the Stickeen Indians will become a happy people.

—Part of a speech by Chief Toyatte, addressed to a packed schoolhouse at Wrangell, as transcribed by Presbyterian missionary Amanda McFarland in 1877. From Polly and Leon Gordon Miller, *The Lost Heritage of Alaska: Adventures and Art of the Alaskan Coastal Indians,* 1967

Vincent Colyer, Special Indian Agent for the United States, visited Alaska in 1869. At Wrangell he observed 32 plank houses on a tongue of land, 500 yards from the government post "with the guns commanding the village." In front of Chief Shakes's house he noted three totem poles (today seen in replicas), describing them as "some very curious colossal frogs, a bear, war-chief, with his 'big medicine dance hat' on." Colyer here refers to Shakes V, also known as Wolf 18.

Over the next few years the U.S. Army tried to control uncooperative Alaska Natives through cruelty. They "administered bombardments like righteous spankings," wrote art historians Polly and Leon Miller. Once, for example, a Kake and a Chilkat wanted to leave the village at Sitka to chop wood. A sentry shot them. In revenge, the Kakes killed two prospectors. General Jeff Davis then ordered the Saginaw to Kake Island, where it bombarded and destroyed the 16 houses of Old Kake and two other villages, plus canoes and food stored for winter. Some months later Wrangell was bombarded for various offenses—for one, a white laundress had had her finger bitten off.

For the most part, Wrangell was a sleepy little place. That all changed when strikes in the Cassiar District of British Columbia, 300 miles inland, brought a stampede of prospectors, all of whom needed provisions and tools—as well as recreation in saloons and brothels. In 1874 about 3,000 newcomers headed up the Stikine River to the Cassiar. By 1877 the army fort was abandoned. Meanwhile, the three Stikine chiefs—Shakes V, Toyatte, and Shustaks—began requesting schools and churches. Their pleas were answered the following year by Presbyterian missionaries Amanda McFarland and S. Hall Young.

Naturalist John Muir went ashore in July 1879. On one hand Muir criticized Wrangell as "a rough place" laid out with "devil-may-care abandon," but on the other he delighted in the profusion of wild berries, the community's affection for children, and the tranquility. "I never heard a noisy brawl in the streets or a clap of thunder," he wrote, "and the waves seldom spoke much above a whisper along the beach. . . . The cloudless days are calm, pearl-gray, and brooding in tone, inclining to rest and peace; the islands seem to drowse and float on the glassy water, and in the woods scarce a leaf stirs."

By 1880 steamers began running direct routes from Victoria, British Columbia, to Wrangell—but only every few weeks or so. Another wave of prospectors scrambled through in 1898 on their way to the Klondike. Industry took root; two canneries and a sawmill opened, and a newspaper, the Wrangell *Sentinel*, began publishing in 1902.

Visitors to Wrangell in 1911 photographed themselves with totems and shopped along a wharf lined with Stikine women selling baskets. In the yard of the sawmill stood the abandoned plank house of Chief Kadashan, a man described by missionary Young as "the shrewdest and most diplomatic of the Stikeens . . . and a master of metaphors." Tourists hired a canoe to cross the slough separating the Native graveyard from Shakes Island. For half a dollar Shakes himself, 56, admitted visitors to his private museum and described the uses of the objects displayed there.

KID STUFF

- When the tide ebbs below the 12-foot level, treasure-hunt for the dozens of original petroglyphs on **Petroglyph Beach.** Cast-stone reproductions of several petroglyphs have been installed on the stairs to the beach so they can be viewed at high tide. Rubbings can be made of these casts—*not* the originals.

- The **Wrangell Community Church of God** (212 Bennett St.; skating rink, 907/874–2259) hosts a roller rink in its basement. Call for hours.

- Take a mineral soak at **Chief Shakes Hot Springs,** 28 miles NW. There are dressing rooms, benches and outhouses. Coastal Island Charters (907/874–2014) can get you there.

WRANGELL NOW *map page 52*

A loud exhalation sounds over the water. It draws the eye to blowhole mist a mile away. In a few seconds a humpback whale reveals the sleek curve of its back. More exhalations follow, almost like echoes. It's a pod of three females, one with her calf swimming close beside her, often sliding skin-to-skin against her for reassurance.

This scene is common near Wrangell and elsewhere along the Inside Passage. Humpbacks may travel in family groups of eight or more, sometimes blowing and feeding side by side like a marine chorus line. Today's visitors can record in their travel diaries many of the same vistas and species of wildlife that Muir and his friend Young recorded over a century ago.

Populations grow slowly in Southeast Alaska. In 1967 the Bureau of Indian Affairs counted a city population of 1,500, including 1,000 Tlingits. Wrangell nearly topped 3,000 in 2005, but Natives now make up only roughly a quarter of the population. Wrangell plays host to just one 900-person paddlewheeler a week for two months. As a result, the town feels mellow and unhurried even in high season. At the ferry dock, town children sell locally gathered garnets from muffin tins. The town's museum unlocks its doors only Tuesday through Saturday or when a paddlewheeler or ferry glides into port. Wrangell is also drier than most of Southeast, with an average annual rainfall of 80 inches.

Wrangell draws less than 1% of cruise traffic, compared with Juneau's 95% share. However, Wrangell, Petersburg, and Coffman Cove have teamed up to market themselves as the Alaska Rainforest Islands, connected by the Inter-Island Ferry. It's an attractive transportation option for those who find the bigger ports too much of a good thing.

For an off-the-beaten-deck visit to Wrangell, consider the 55-passenger MS *Sheltered Seas* (Alaska Sightseeing Cruise West; 800/426–7702). This day boat offers intimate excursions from Juneau to Wrangell and other cozy destinations, like Petersburg.

WALKING TOUR

Pick up a walking map at the **Wrangell Chamber of Commerce/Visitors Center** (224 Front St.; 907/874–3901; www.wrangellchamber.org) near the cruise-ship docks. The **Wrangell Museum** (2906 Outer Dr.; 907/874–3770) shares a building with the James & Elsie Nolan Civic Center. The museum focuses on the town's history from the prehistoric era through the missionary period. Note the photos of the original Shakes Tribal House and of Shakes VII at a 1940 potlatch. Of particular interest are four house posts dating from the late 1700s and believed to be the oldest surviving Tlingit house posts. Intricate spruce-root and cedar-

Wrangell's mellow harbor.

TOTEM POLES

Captain James Cook was among the first Europeans to see the magnificent Northwest signpost, the totem pole. Unlike most newcomers to the area, Cook had a rare appreciation for Native art and did not condemn it as "pagan." He surmised that totems were "images of some of their ancestors whom they venerate as divinities," coming close to the truth. It was hard to ignore totems 40 feet high, facing the shore as if to say "private property." Essentially the totem is a legal document in wood. It reminds residents of legends, great chiefs, clan lineage, and claimed territory.

Totems are traditionally red cedar, carved with tools of stone, shell, beaver tooth, and jade. The art of the totem reached its peak in the 1800s, when steel tools were introduced and the wealth from fur trading urged chiefs to compete in commissioning totems.

Tsimshian poles are known for their sense of scale and proportion, precision, and sculptural technique. Details are rendered in low relief rather than by surface lines. Crests include the sea bear and whale. Color is used sparingly.

Haida poles use deeply cut, unpainted, dramatic forms that overlap and interlock. Haida crests include the seal, eagle, killer whale, and frog. Figures are static, as though freeze-framed.

Tlingit poles show a series of separated, superimposed, realistic forms. A watchman figure or clan crest may be placed at the top. Attached, projecting pieces such as an eagle's wings or a raven's beak are signature devices. Figures are dynamic, portrayed climbing, sticking out a tongue, or flying. Color is used extensively—traditionally black, blue-green, red, and yellow. Paints were created from pulverized minerals or charcoal, with a fillip of fish eggs as a fixative.

Outside, Americans first saw totem poles during the Centennial Exhibition in Philadelphia in 1876. But by 1900, as Native communities and folkways began to fray under the pressure of prospectors, educators, and settlers, wood carving was on the decline. Missionaries set fire to poles when tribes were away hunting or fishing, or forced converts to demonstrate their conversion by burning poles and traditional regalia.

Public works projects and the World's Fair displays in the 1930s helped to rekindle interest in totem poles, as did a Haines carving workshop founded after World War II. Totems today are typically created on commission for a public building like the Smithsonian's new Native American Museum or in commemoration of an event.

Ancient, mysterious etchings on
the namesake Petroglyph Beach.

BASICS ON BEARS

The Inside Passage has thriving bear populations—both brown and black. Bears were some of the first large mammals to populate this vast wilderness after the ice sheets retreated. Remains of giant prehistoric bears in caves in Southeast Alaska have been carbon dated to 14,000 to 16,000 years ago, indicating that there were a few ice-free spots along the coast.

The brown bear, *Ursus arctos*, has thick fur that varies from dark chocolate-brown to blond as a showgirl. Also known as a grizzly, the brown bear is distinguished by a muscular hump at the shoulders, a dished face, and a large head. It is larger and has longer, straighter claws than the black bear. Coastal brownies with plenty of food in their habitat can grow to 1,400 pounds and stand over nine feet tall when they rise up out of tundra brush—a truly scary sight. Brown bears live on Admiralty, Baranof, and Chichagof islands as well as on the mainland.

Mature black bears average less than half the size of brownies—only 180 to 200 pounds. *Ursus americanus* is common all over North America. Black bears have short, curved claws and straight faces; their ears are bigger, and they're better at climbing trees than brownies. Like the brown bear, the black bear varies in color—from hematite-black to cinnamon-brown. There are 17,000 blackies concealed in Inside Passage forests. Those who venture from dense cover into human neighborhoods often develop a liking for the sweet syrup in hummingbird feeders, black-oil sunflower seeds, cracked corn, and dog kibble. In Juneau, special bear-proof trash containers prevent raids.

The glacier or "blue" bear is a rare blue-gray color phase of the black bear. Its fur varies from a dirty white to black with many gray hairs and even overtones of green or silver. The first one was bagged near Yakutat in 1906, and few others have ever been seen.

Generally, black and brown bears do not mix in the same habitat. Both brown and

bark baskets date to 1900. Trapping, fishing, mining and forest industries are represented in the collection. Don't fret; if you're in town on a Sunday or Monday; the museum graciously opens by appointment.

A brown bear sow leads two cubs along the coast.

black bears can swim, although neither can swim as well as the polar bear. Both have flattened molars for grinding plants such as roots and skunk cabbage shoots.

Outside the museum, turn right on Front Street, pausing to examine the four totems at Kiksetti Totem Park. Front Street soon becomes Shakes Street, leading to the boardwalk to ★ **Shakes Island**. Cross to the island to visit the **Tribal**

House of the Bear, a site open based on tourist demand and by appointment (Wrangell Cooperative Assn., 907/874–3747). The tribal house is a 1939–40 replica of the original 1834 structure, erected with hand-adzed boards, without nails; the house posts are replicas of the four originals in the museum, carved without power tools. I found Shakes Island particularly moody when I visited alone, at night, in a heavy drizzle. The seven totems loomed like giants in the gray mist, and I almost expected them to move.

Two of them are replicas of totems carved in the late 1800s—totems that figure prominently in late-19th-century photo albums. The Bear-up-the-Mountain Totem with its unique bear footprints commemorates Shakes's ancestors and a grizzly who led them to safety on the highest ground in the area during a great flood. The Gonakadet Totem is a memorial pole, carved as a final resting place for the ashes of Chief Shakes VI's parents. Gonakadet is a legendary lake monster whose magic skin was stolen by a young man to satisfy his greedy mother-in-law.

Head back toward the dock, taking a right on St. Michael's Street and then a left on Church Street. The **St. Rose of Lima Church** (c. 1897) is the seat of Alaska's oldest Roman Catholic parish. A little farther along, take a gander at the four Civilian Conservation Corps-carved totems on the grounds of the **Irene Ingle Public Library** (Second and Bevier Sts.).

For a vista of downtown, head up Bevier Street and turn right on Cassair Street. Climb the stairs leading to Third Street, which makes a couple of right turns to the **Mt. Dewey trailhead.** The hike to the top is quite easy; at 400 feet Mt. Dewey is hardly a mountain. After taking in the view, head back down to Second Street, turn right and then right again on Stikine Avenue, which parallels the shore of Zimovia Strait. About half a mile out of town stands an information kiosk at ★**Petroglyph Beach,** a State Historic Park. The beach has one of the largest concentrations of petroglyphs along the Pacific Coast—about 40 of these ancient rock etchings. Look for spirals, big eyes, heart-shaped faces, and fish pecked into the faces of rocks facing seaward, near the high-tide line. No one knows the age of these petroglyphs, but they were presumably prehistoric territorial signs for canoes exploring the beach. Those messages were probably sentiments like "This is our beach; no trespassing; catch your salmon elsewhere."

This entire walk will take three or four hours.

BRIEF EXCURSIONS

Want to stretch those hamstrings? **Rainwalker Expeditions** (Second and Evergreen Sts.; 907/874–3012) rents bikes and helmets. A 6-mile paved walking and biking path runs from downtown to the trailhead for Rainbow Falls at Shoemaker Bay. If you stay at Fennimore's B&B you can use a bicycle free.

Take a hike. The **Rainbow Falls Trail,** just under a mile, is moderately steep. The 3½-mile **Institute Creek Trail** begins roughly half a mile up the Rainbow Falls Trail. Occasional muskeg (swamp) is bridged by boardwalks. You might see wildflowers like bog laurel and marsh marigold. There's a steep and muddy stretch, but persist and you'll be rewarded with Shoemaker Overlook, where you'll have panoramas of Zimovia Strait and Shoemaker Bay.

Wrangell offers the only USGA–rated golf course in Southeast Alaska. However, the 9-hole course, **Muskeg Meadows** (Ishiyama Rd.; 907/874–4653) has views of the ocean and mountain that may distract duffers from their game. Forgive me if I don't use phrases like "natural beauty" or "pristine wilderness" again, but trust me, it's here.

LONGER OUTINGS

★**Anan Creek Bear Observatory** (800/367–9745) is one of the state's best places to see bears at close range from a relatively safe vantage point. Anan Creek is an ancient Tlingit fishing site with a large pink salmon run during July and August. Attracted by fat, juicy pinks and steelhead trout, black bears and the occasional brownie come to the creek to fish. (The fish draw seals, bald eagles, and ravens, too.) The observatory is 35 miles south of Wrangell by plane or boat charter. You can view bears from an observation platform above the creek and a three-sided blind closer to the falls. Visitors are closely watched in turn by Forest Service personnel. No food is allowed on the trails or in the viewing areas, and flash photography is discouraged. Anan Creek is a very exclusive excursion. Only 60 visitors are allowed each day in July and August. Permits ($10) are available from the Forest Service office in Wrangell (907/874–2323). You can make it a day trip via plane with Sunrise Aviation (800/874–2311; $150 per person) or via boat with either Alaska Peak & Seas (907/874–2454; $190 per person) or Alaska Charters & Adventures (907/874–4157; $158 per person). Don't expect the bears at rainy Anan to swat salmon out of the air like a circus act. The key items to bring are good boots, rain gear, and patience.

Wrangell has 100 miles of forest roads to explore by hiking, mountain bike, or recreational vehicle. Pick up trail and mountain-bike information at the U.S. Forest Service Ranger Station (525 Bennett St.; 907/874–2323).

Follow the Stikine River into the **Stikine-LeConte Wilderness.** The wilderness has the world's second-largest concentration of eagles during spring spawning runs. Other birds include whistling swans, sandhill cranes, and mergansers. The small, tasty, oily hooligan, which also run in spring, rate high on the food pyramid of gulls and Steller sea lions, too. Moose, bears, and migrating waterfowl are plentiful, and from one spot on the river, you can see 21 glaciers. Breakaway Adventures (3 Mile Zimovia Hwy.; 888/385–2488) offers all-day trips into the territory, with a stop at Chief Shakes Hot Springs as a bonus. For something noisier, Alaska Waters (907/874–2378) runs five-hour jet-boat trips on the Stikine. A spectacular feature of the river is the 55-mile Grand Canyon of the Stikine, about 200 miles upriver. For kayaking or canoeing the Stikine, see the Forest Service guide available from the Wrangell Ranger District (525 Bennett St.; 907/874–2323).

Author, photographer, and former park ranger Karen Jettmar offers terrific outings with her **Equinox Wilderness Expeditions** (604/222–1219; www.equinox expeditions.com). The trips, which include time for reflection and solitude, are eco-friendly and timed to coincide with annual migrations. The nine-day Icy Bay expedition heads into Wrangell-St. Elias National Park. Equinox was named one of the 55 Best Adventure Operations on the Planet by *National Geographic Travel* magazine in 2007.

FAVORITE PLACES TO SHOP AND EAT

Owner Olga Norris "took the chance" to open **Norris Gift Shop** (124 Front St., 907/874–3810) in 1970 to market her own oils and watercolors. Since then she's branched out into three-foot signed totems carved in Ketchikan, gold nugget and Arctic opal jewelry, ivory and bone carvings, Alaska Spice Co. teas, handmade cedar or maple bowls, and Israel Shotridge Christmas ornaments in shapes like Tlingit drums.

One tasty souvenir to target at Norris and elsewhere is syrup from **Birch Boy Products** (907/767–5660; www.birchboy.com). Birch Boy, a company based in Haines, bottles more than 20 natural elixirs that make delectable pours for waffles or ice cream. The most unusual may be birch, but they also distill spruce tip, rhubarb, highbush cranberry, and Russian-American cherry (based on sour cherries planted in Sitka by Russian settlers).

Zak's Café. Katherine George-Byrd and her hubby opened this steak and chop house in 2001, and serve up stir fries, pasta, and seafood as well as beef. Sandwiches, salads, and wraps are popular at lunch. In the evening, most diners opt for the halibut, which you can get almost any way you want it: grilled, battered and deep fried, in a wrap, or blackened. The dining room is decorated with objects the couple has collected on travels to Jamaica and Mexico, so that halibut might be served up on a Mexican placemat. *316 Front St., 907/874–3355.* **$–$$**

A fishing boat pushes through the Wrangell Narrows, near Petersburg.

PETERSBURG

The 21st-century's supersized cruise ships are too broad in the beam to sail the channel leading to Petersburg, making this beautiful, little town perfect for an excursion off the beaten path. In fact, Petersburg is so "out there" that it lacks home mail-delivery service. At the northern tip of Mitkof Island and about three hours (50 miles) from Wrangell by ferry, Petersburg bills itself the "Heart of the Inside Passage." The island's highest point is Crystal Mountain, a 3,317-foot peak rising above land that is mostly muskeg, the arctic term for "swamp." Muskeg is mossy, soggy wetland carpeted with heather, buckbean, and stands of scraggly jack pine.

Mitkof Island is separated from Kupreanof Island by the 20-mile-long Wrangell Narrows. Portions of the Narrows are just wide enough to accommodate a state ferry. Girdled by this tight channel, tides slosh back and forth vigorously, varying as much as 23 feet in a day. It's a thrilling ride, giving boaters the sense they could touch the banks on either side.

PETERSBURG THEN

Place names in the Petersburg area provide clues to its recent history. Duncan Canal, an inlet on Kupreanof Island, was named in 1793 by George Vancouver for an officer in the Royal Navy. Kupreanof Island, which forms the west shore of Wrangell Narrows, was named for Ivan Antonovich Kupreanof, the seventh chief manager of the Russian-American Company. Popular tourist destinations LeConte Bay and LeConte Glacier were named in 1887 for a geology professor at the University of California. Froot Loop Road is a 20th-century addition.

Tlingits maintained a fish camp here 2,000 years ago, and the abundance of fish also drew Norwegian immigrant Peter Buschmann to pick this as a spot for a cannery in 1897. Buschmann, an employee of Icy Straits Packing Company, soon had the surrounding glades ringing with the sound of pilings being driven for a wharf. In 1898 Buschmann installed a sawmill to churn out the lumber needed for the cannery (completed in 1900). During its first season Icy Straits packed 32,750 cases of salmon. As the cannery flourished, summer-season workers decided to remain year-round. Homes and businesses sprang up around the cannery, many of them owned by Norwegians. A competitor, the Pacific Coast & Norway Packing, opened a saltery six miles south of Petersburg in 1900, and built a cannery the following year. On the strength of all this canning, Petersburg

FAQs

What is a "highliner"?

A skilled seine (net) fisherman, one who actually turns a profit.

What is "pulp" and what is made from it?

Straight logs are milled into boards, veneer, plywood, shingles, and shakes. (They are also called "mill" logs or "round" logs.) Crooked or damaged logs are ground into pulp—the cellulose equivalent of mashed potato. This mash is processed into paper, cardboard, cellophane, photographic film, and synthetic fabrics such as rayon and Tencel.

What is a rookery?

Usually the word means a breeding place or colony of European crows (rooks). In Alaska the word is used to describe colonies of nesting puffins, other gregarious sea birds such as kittiwakes, auklets and murres, or Steller sea lions. It is often a small, rocky, isolated island or cliff, preferred because there are no predators (fox, human, or otherwise) to disturb young ones. Prince of Wales is noted for its sea bird rookeries.

The Sons of Norway Hall hosts bazaars, rosemaling classes, and *lutefisk* dinners.

PETERSBURG

Alaska State Ferry route.
To Juneau

0   250   500 Feet

Blader   St

First

Wrangell Narrows

Charles   St

High School

St

Swimming Pool

Sandy Beach

Dolphin   St

Second

Third

Fifth

NorQuest Seafood
Cannery

Excel   St

Excel   St

Cruise Ship Terminal

Way

Rd

Fourth

St

Petersburg
Medical Center

North Boat
Harbor

Harbor

Fram   St

Clausen Memorial
Museum

Fram   St

Visitor Information/
Chamber of Commerce

St

St

Chief John
Lott St

Gjoa   St

Gjoa   St

Sing Lee
Alley

To
Airport, 1 mi.

Viking Ship Replica

Federal Building: Forest Service

To
Falls Creek Fish Ladder, 9 mi.
Swan Observatory, 16 mi.
Crystal Lake Hatchery, 16.5 mi.
Three Lakes Loop Rd, 19 mi.

Haugen   Dr

City Hall

Hammer's Slough

Harbormaster Office/
Showers/Restrooms

Sons of
Norway Hall

Bojer-Wikan
Fisherman's
Memorial Park

Birch St Boardwalk

Ira II   St

S. Fourth St

To
Ferry Dock,
South Boat Harbor &
Middle Boat Harbor

Nordic Dr

Hammer's Slough
Historical Area

Petersburg keeps close ties to its fishing-hub and Norwegian-immigrant past.

was incorporated in 1910. Six years later, NorQuest Seafoods built Alaska's first shrimp cannery at Petersburg. Tourists began arriving on a regular basis in 1912, when the Citizen Wharf Company built a dock and terminal for steamships.

PETERSBURG NOW *map page 71*

Norwegian was once commonly spoken along Petersburg's wooden streets, and the influence of Norway lingers. As you walk around town, you'll see blond braids, gartered kneesocks, rosemaling (a type of decorative painting often applied to house fronts and shutters), and street names like "Gjoa." The Leikarring Dancers put on spirited performances at the Sons of Norway Hall. There's a local taste for *lutefisk* (dried cod) and catered smorgasbords at weddings. For the Little Norway Festival on Syttende Mai (May 17, Norwegian Constitution Day) and again on July 4, locals pull out their old family recipes to make traditional Norwegian dishes such as *krumkake* (a crisp, wafflelike cookie rolled into a cylinder and filled with whipped cream) and *fattigmann* ("poor man's cake," a fried sweet pastry). All this Scandinavian atmosphere has earned the picturesque town the nickname "Little Norway."

As is true for the majority of Inside Passage communities, Petersburg doesn't lack for rain. The average annual precipitation is 110 inches, with half of that

A replica Viking ship makes a perfect photo op.

Visit Hammer Slough at high tide to see the historic buildings reflected in the water.

descending from October through December. To blend in with the 3,200 locals, just tug on a pair of X-tra Tuff boots and hitch your rain pants to rainbow suspenders.

Today Petersburg Medical Center is the town's largest employer, with federal, state, and local governments not far behind. Nevertheless, Petersburg remains a fishing town. Salmon is the main catch, but halibut, black cod, shrimp, herring, and crab (Dungeness, king, and tanner) are also strong fishery players. (Petersburg is also nicknamed the "halibut capital of Alaska.") Some fishermen are diversifying into geoduck, abalone, and sea cucumbers. Today the NorQuest Seafoods plant processes marine edibles ranging from shrimp and salmon to rockfish and sea urchins or "sea eggs." For fishing licenses or details about hooking into a "barn door" (large halibut), head to the Alaska Department of Fish and Game (16 Sing Lee Alley; 907/772–3801).

Petersburg-based activities include whale-watching in Frederick Sound or kayaking among the seals near LeConte Glacier (25 miles east). For details about humpback whale–watching, helicopter flightseeing, guided kayak tours, or glacier outings, consult Viking Travel (800/327–2571), Whale Song Cruises (907/772–9393), and Tongass Kayak Adventures (907/772–4600). Since 2002, the Inter-Island Ferry (866/308–4848) has offered trips between Hollis and Ketchikan daily, and trips between Coffman Cove, Wrangell, and Petersburg three days a week in summer.

Anxious to check your e-mail? The Public Library, above the Fire Hall, offers free Internet access. The library is on Nordic Drive, between Haugen Drive and Birch Street.

Ships tie up at several locations—some at the south harbor near Sing Lee Alley; some at the fueling dock; and others in the north harbor. The town is so compact that there's no "main drag." Begin at the **Petersburg Visitor Information Center** (corner of First and Fram streets; 907/772–4636 or 866/484–4700) for brochures and video presentations. Turn right on Fram Street, walking past the Medical Center to the **Clausen Memorial Museum** (203 Fram St.; 907/772–3598). Videos and demos by curators detail how to catch a salmon or bait a crab pot. Displays illustrate the area's history with such artifacts as a 200-year-old Tlingit canoe from this region, carved yellow-cedar halibut hooks, and a stuffed 126½-pound king salmon caught in 1939. On the grounds, take a gander at the huge fish-trap anchors as well as the abstract aluminum *Fisk* sculpture by artist Carson Boysen.

Head back along Fram Street toward Wrangell Narrows, and turn left on Main Street/Nordic Drive. In a couple of blocks you'll reach **Hammer Slough,** where buildings perch on pilings above the water. At high tide the weathered structures are reflected in the Slough. At the entrance to the Slough is the **Sons of Norway Hall** (Sing Lee Alley; 907/772–4575), begun by Peter Buschmann in 1897. Decorated with rosemaling, the hall jumps during the Little Norway Festival and the King Salmon Derby, both in May. You might want to stop next door at **Sing Lee Alley Books** (907/772–4440) for its Alaskana. Near the hall is **Bojer-Wikan Fisherman's Memorial Park,** which commemorates local residents lost at sea. Birch Street Boardwalk parallels the Slough on one bank, with the Hammer Slough Historic Area on the other bank. For a taste of local entertainment, drop into **Kito's Kave** (Sing Lee Alley; 907/772–3207) for live music, Mexican food, and Alaska beer.

Next, turn back to Nordic Drive and walk north several blocks to **Eagle's Roost Park,** where you'll have a good chance of seeing a bald eagle, especially in early summer. Continue on Nordic Drive to the Hungry Point View Area, which has views of the Coast Mountains and the peak of Devil's Thumb. Here Nordic Drive becomes Sandy Beach Road. You can turn onto Hungry Point Trail, a 40-minute walk where black-tailed deer hang out. The trail will lead you back to town. Or you may choose to walk farther on Sandy Beach Road to the beach access at the **Whale Observatory.** Here mounted binoculars help you scan the ocean for flukes and spouts, and interpretive signs provide info on marine mammals such as humpbacks and orcas.

OF FLIPPERS AND FLUKES

The Inside Passage's most common whale species are the humpback and the orca (killer whale). Whales are usually spotted when surfacing to exhale through dorsal blowholes. The exhale is mixed with water vapor, and is often visible from afar.

A humpback is a leviathan—45 to 50 feet long. Most of its body is dark gray, but its throat is creamy white. It has long pale flippers at its sides, and a huge, horizontal fluke or tail. When the fluke flips high into the air, the humpback is usually angling into the ocean for a long, deep dive.

Humpbacks put thousands of miles on their inner odometers each year. They spend winter in the warm waters around the Hawaiian Islands or Baja, Mexico, where female humpbacks give birth. As spring arrives, the whales migrate north to spend the summer in the feeding grounds off Alaska. The female humpbacks often swim in protective pods with their calves.

These enormous creatures feed on krill (tiny, shrimplike organisms) and small fish. Humpbacks are baleen whales, so called for the horny, fringed plates that dangle from their upper jaws. The hair-like fringe acts as a strainer, separating food from seawater. Humpbacks may cooperate in a chorus line of six to eight, feeding side by side. Their most spectacular behavior is bubble-net feeding, in which they lunge up through the water, exhaling a curtain of bubbles that confuses and concentrates small fish. As the humpback reaches the surface, it explodes into the air, gulping down the fleeing fish. Another signature humpback move is "breaching"—leaping into the air and slamming down on the water's surface. No one's sure why humpbacks breach; it could be a form of play. Humpbacks are also known for "singing." In winter, male humpbacks can emit complex patterns of sound for several hours at a stretch, while in summer they produce short tunes lasting only a minute or so.

The sleek, muscular orca, meanwhile, is a toothed whale with distinctive black and white markings. Orcas are usually about half the length of humpbacks, and they stay in the ocean off Alaska year-round. The orca is a powerful swimmer and can travel a hundred miles in a day. Males, known as bulls, have large dorsal fins up to six feet tall. The stiffness of the fin indicates the health of the whale.

Orcas generally travel in small pods and will hunt cooperatively, strategizing to capture prey and sharing their catches. Like humpbacks, orcas will spyhop and breach.

Drop by the Whale Observatory to look for passing humpbacks.

This walk will take several hours—or most of a day, depending on how long you spend in the museum, bookstore, park, or bar.

BRIEF EXCURSIONS

Bird-watch at the ★Swan Observatory (Mile 16, Mitkof Hwy.; no phone), a shielded place, or "blind," from which to view trumpeter swans. Dozens of these big, beautiful waterfowl spend the winter on Mitkof Island, and hundreds more take a break here between mid-October and early December while migrating south. In summer, bears and salmon splash in the shallow water downriver from the observatory.

If you're archaeologically curious, sign up for a tour with a U.S. Forest Service guide to see petroglyphs and prehistoric Tlingit fish traps on ★Petroglyph Beach. The petroglyphs, showing heart-shaped faces with circular eyes and mouths, are on a large rock outcrop. Nearby, visible at low tide, are the remains of five heart-shaped wood-stake fish traps. The oldest traps are two stone struc-

KID STUFF

- First, buy a horned Viking helmet and a wooden sword at **Kinder Komfort** (15 Sing Lee Alley; 907/772–4100). Then head to Bojer-Wikan Fisherman's Memorial Park and board the *Valhalla*. With its striped sail and fiddlehead prow, the ship provides a memorable photo op.

- Sign up for a **rosemaling class** at the Cubby Hole (14 Sing Lee Alley; 907/772–2717). Rosemaling is a Norwegian decorative art of painted or carved floral designs; it translates as "rose painting." Classes are geared to all ages, and you usually paint on wood.

- Kids under 12 can **fish off the dock** without a fishing license. It's possible to catch herring or Dolly Varden.

- **Enter a local contest** for a shot at a $2,000 first prize: guess how many one-pound cans of salmon will be packed in Petersburg in the current season. Tickets are sold July 1 to August 21 at 907/772–4294; the winner is announced during Seafood Fest in October.

tures—one on either side of the beach—that are nearly 3,000 years old. Over 30 feet across, the traps led fish at high tide into a maze of two overlapping circles. As the tide ebbed, fish were caught in the maze. Tlingits could then spear the fish or gather them by hand. You can also see remnants of five later traps fashioned from hemlock stakes pounded into the sand—a type of fish trap found nowhere else in the world. These are about 2,000 years old. The Forest Service shares an office with the Visitor Information Center (corner of First and Fram streets; 907/772–3871).

Interested in an introduction to a noisy, gooey "slime line"? Cannery tours supply an up-close look at fish processing. **Tonka Seafoods** offers hour-long tours (22 Sing Lee Alley; 888/560–3662; www.tonkaseafoods.com). The forces of fish and bleach do battle at fish processing plants, providing a damp but not unpleasant milieu. Tonka is a small, intimate operation; on a big day they process 2,000 pounds. The owners act as tour guides, explaining the basics of the seafood industry, and then taking you into the main workroom where fish are beheaded and gutted. Samples of dip or lox are free at the close of the tour.

WALKING, WADING, CLIMBING, SLITHERING

The small island was an unlimited world. I was never bored. It was a thrill just walking in the woods, for the aimless jaunts always seemed to lead to discoveries. I was forever learning something new about nature or myself. Both I came to realize as being one and the same. The external world reflects our internal composition: a circulatory system of streams and rivers, a sensitive skin of earth, mountain spines, stones as bones, breathing in the surf, hair on grassy headlands. The Indians regarded the earth as a living entity—a human system on a grand scale. And the resemblance went as far as psychological forces finding release as birds, trees, whales, and the weather. As Gary Snyder wrote, "Outwardly, the equivalent of the subconscious is the wilderness."

. . . To make my way, I walked, waded, climbed, and now dropped to hands and knees, or in tight spots slithered through on my belly. As I went further in, I saw cedar trees that had grown immense, nearly as giant as their redwood cousins. Overhead, their broad canopies closed out sunlight . . . .

The high tree needles and leaves tapered to points that pierced the rain. Water fell in long drops, penetrating deep into mossy beds. Gurgling rivulets of water cut channels through the layered loam. Even the rocks looked as soft and porous as sponges. The air was rich with decay. The smell wasn't putrid but had a clean yeasty odor that expanded in the lungs.

—Michael Modzelewski, *Inside Passage: Living with Killer Whales, Bald Eagles, and Kwakiutl Indians,* 1991

If you're interested in fish raising, head out to **Crystal Lake Fish Hatchery** (Mile 17, Mitkof Hwy.; 907/772–4772). The hatchery raises 1.5 million king salmon and 150,000 cohos. Most are released right there, although some are taken to Anita Bay near Wrangell and some to Neets Bay outside Ketchikan. A visit here is a do-it-yourself excursion—you walk around 24 outdoor tanks called "raceways." It's fun to watch when food pellets are tossed over the surface of the raceways and the water boils in feeding frenzy. The most exciting time to visit is July and August, when adult cohos return and can be seen through glass windows in the fish ladder.

Cathy Harris, owner of the Cubby Hole, demonstrates rosemaling.

Take a stroll along the **Blind River Rapids Trail,** 14 miles from downtown off the Mitkof Highway. A quarter-mile boardwalk leads to the rapids, passing over a muskeg. It's an easy half-hour walk, but you may want to linger for several hours because this spot offers one of the few opportunities in the Inside Passage to fish from shore for king salmon during June and July. (The visitors' center maintains a list of local outfitters.) The boardwalk is handicapped accessible, as are restrooms and a shelter at trail's end.

Fly over ★LeConte Glacier, which squats on the mainland between town and the Stikine River. It's the southernmost active tidewater glacier in North America, often calving bergs into the 15-mile-long fjord named Frederick Sound. Occasionally bergs float onto Petersburg beaches or into the boat harbors. LeConte's icefield has shrunk about 100 feet since a 1948 aerial survey. For flight-seeing, contact Kupreanof Flying Service (907/772–3396). From above, glaciers are sinuous extrusions ribbed by rock debris and pocked with deep crevasses. Flights last about 45 minutes. Weather is tricky here, so resist urging a pilot to take off if he or she is reluctant.

LONGER OUTINGS

Petersburg is a doorway to the **Tongass National Forest.** The Petersburg Ranger District maintains 20 recreation cabins. Most cabins are accessible by boat or

floatplane only, making them ideal for replenishing your spiritual batteries in the solitude of the wilderness. The Mallard Slough cabin near LeConte Bay can be reserved by applying at the Petersburg Ranger District front desk, through the National Recreation Reservation Service (877/444–6777; www.reserveusa.com).

There are no Forest Service cabins in LeConte Bay. However, the Ranger District provides a cabin that meets barrier-free standards: the Kah Sheets Lake Cabin. It can be reached

Tonka Seafoods can introduce you to a "slime line."

by way of a 2½-mile boardwalk from Kah Sheets Bay. A rowboat is provided for sockeye fishing.

Listen to humpback whales sing on a cabin-cruiser trip with Captain Ron Loesch of **Whale Song Cruises** (907/772–9393; www.whalesongcruises.com). The cruiser's aluminum hull magnifies underwater sounds, making it possible to hear the haunting calls. Trips usually include Frederick Sound, Five Finger Lighthouse, and a sea lion rookery.

Take a weeklong **guided kayak tour of the Tongass with Tongass Kayak Adventures** (907/772–4600; www.tongasskayak.com). This isn't a marathon paddling situation, but you should be in good shape. You'll take kayaking day trips out of a fixed camp, poking around and seeing cool stuff like icebergs and waterfalls in crannies of LeConte Bay. All guides are naturalists.

Ride a power boat to LeConte Glacier, then hop into a **kayak for a closer look at the ice with Viking Travel** (800/327–2571). The 10-hour excursions are for a minimum of three people.

FAVORITE PLACES TO SHOP

Wild Celery (400 North Nordic Dr., 907/772–2471) specializes in art by Petersburg residents working with watercolor, beads, ceramics, and wood, among other media.

On Alaska's islands, supermarkets double for the Outside's department stores. You can usually find fishing licenses alongside the milk and bread. The same runs true for clothing stores, which may also carry outdoor gear and guns. If you're looking for a warm Norwegian or Icelandic sweater, **Lee's Clothing** (212 Nordic Dr.; 907/772–4229) is the place. And then there's the grocery department.

FAVORITE PLACES TO EAT

Rooney's Northern Lights Restaurant. This eatery, perched on pilings overlooking the harbor, serves three meals, family style. Seafood offerings vary from day to day, depending on what the owner covets at the processor. He buys his shrimp right at the dock. Scampi, halibut sandwiches and wraps, and shrimp quesadillas are menu regulars. *203 Sing Lee Alley; 907/772–2900.* **$–$$**

Tina's Kitchen. Her kitchen is in a trailer and diners sit in a fully enclosed, heated tent. You can opt for the special, Korean-style beef, or try the fresh salmon burgers, chicken teriyaki, grilled pork tacos, or double-barreled Burrito Supreme. *204 Main St./Nordic Dr., 907/772–2090.* **$–$$**

Get a lift (and a great view) from the Mount Roberts Tramway.

J U N E A U

Juneau is a gem in a magnificent setting—most dazzling on a clear evening when its lights twinkle. It lies on the inland side of Gastineau Channel. Viewed from the harbor, two precipitous, deeply gullied mountains seem to rise directly from the shallow cup that holds downtown. These mounts are Juneau and Roberts.

The city lies near the head of navigation for Gastineau Channel, as, at low tide, the flat coming from either shore leaves only a shallow channel for two miles. Cruise ships penetrating the eight miles from Stephens Passage must perform a 180° turn to exit. Forming the far side of the channel at Juneau's door is Douglas Island, a 20-mile ridge of mountains. The foothills facing downtown Juneau house bedroom communities and schools. Wolves and Sitka deer bound through its forests. The deer are a tiny species—perfect for making a malamute drool.

Juneau is often swathed in climbing mists, with the occasional pea-souper. Even in August, cruise ships approaching via Gastineau Channel sometimes need to sound their fog horns. Juneauites spend many wet days in the knee-high boots, otherwise known as "Southeast sneakers."

JUNEAU THEN

According to Tlingit oral history, the first humans here were the Auk-Kwaan, "lake people." A fish trap unearthed in the muddy bank of Montana Creek in 1991 gives important clues to their arrival. The 700-year-old trap, woven of hemlock and spruce, is the oldest artifact ever found in the Juneau area. Native tradition holds that the Tlingit migrated here 8,000 to 10,000 years ago.

The Auk and Taku Tlingit followed a seasonal round of food-gathering activities. The Auk, for example, had a fish camp on Gastineau Channel when fish were running. The breezes at this site helped dry the fish. In winter they retreated to a more sheltered village near Auk Lake.

This subsistence lifestyle continued undisturbed for centuries. Eventually, however, Western explorers began to probe the nearby waterways as they sought a rumored Northwest Passage connecting the Pacific with the Atlantic. The Spanish cruised the coast first. Then came various British expeditions. At the same time, Russians were gradually establishing settlements as they fanned out from bases to the north and west at Unalaska, Kodiak, Kenai, and Prince William Sound.

Often the Tlingit did not greet these newcomers with open arms. For instance, as the British lieutenant Joseph Whidby explored Lynn Canal for Captain

FAQs

How far are we above sea level?

Juneau is tucked in the back pocket of Gastineau Channel. A century ago, South Franklin Street and Willoughby Avenue were beach where Auk Tlingits pulled their canoes above high tide line. Gradually through the 1920s and '30s, mine tailings created new land. So unless you hike up Mt. Roberts, you're just a few feet above sea level most of the time.

With 222 days of mist and rain, why don't Juneauites use umbrellas?

They go by the drip-dry principle.

Can I drive to Juneau?

Nope. Juneau is the only one of the 50 U.S. capitals that is not connected to the rest of the state's road system. Take a plane or load your vehicle on a ferry. The Alaska Department of Transportation is studying the possibility of a road to Skagway, but hundreds of avalanche chutes and bald eagle nesting sites are in the way. In addition, only half the population of Juneau supports the idea—and much of Skagway opposes it.

How much of Juneau is under ice?

The Juneau Ice Field is North America's fifth largest—larger than Rhode Island—but none of it touches downtown. A century ago, big bergs calved from Mendenhall Glacier regularly floated past downtown. But don't pack an ice axe. Global warming has nipped those bergs in the bud.

Misty, rainy Juneau is sometimes called the "Gateway to the Glaciers."

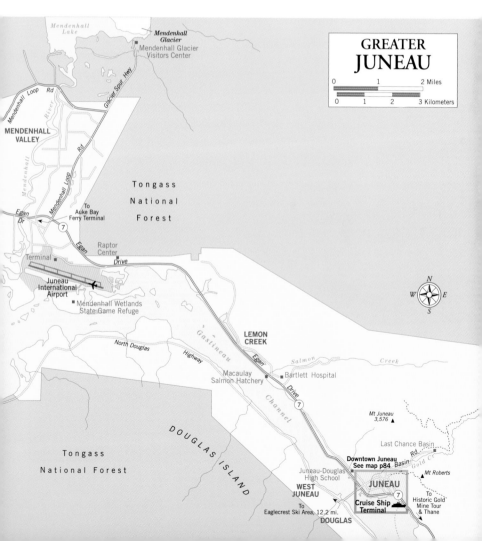

GREATER
JUNEAU

0   1   2 Miles

0   1   2   3 Kilometers

Mendenhall Lake

Mendenhall Glacier

Mendenhall Glacier Visitors Center

Mendenhall Loop Rd

River

MENDENHALL VALLEY

Glacier Spur Hwy

Mendenhall

Mendenhall Loop Rd

Egan Dr

7

To Auke Bay Ferry Terminal

Egan

Raptor Center

Drive

Terminal

Juneau International Airport

Mendenhall Wetlands State Game Refuge

Tongass National Forest

Gastineau

North Douglas Highway

Egan Drive

LEMON CREEK

Salmon Creek

Macaulay Salmon Hatchery

■ Bartlett Hospital

7

Channel

Tongass National Forest

DOUGLAS ISLAND

Mt Juneau 3,576 ▲

Last Chance Basin

Basin Rd

Gold Cr

Mt Roberts ▲

Juneau-Douglas High School

Downtown Juneau See map p84

WEST JUNEAU

JUNEAU

7

To Eaglecrest Ski Area, 12.2 mi.

Cruise Ship Terminal

To Historic Gold Mine Tour & Thane

DOUGLAS

George Vancouver in July 1794, a large canoe approached bearing a chief who made Whidby a present of a sea-otter skin. The chief was magnificently dressed in a Chilkat blanket and a copper and brass "crown" from which ermine skins dangled. The following day several other British canoes arrived, and the chief's attitude became less cordial. He attempted to board the yawl, apparently to plunder it. Whidby escaped from these Natives—probably Auks—and came to a place which Vancouver named Berners Bay, 40 miles from modern Juneau's downtown. As they navigated Favorite Channel, they saw smoke and Tlingit in various directions; in Gastineau Channel Natives threatened them again.

After circumnavigating Admiralty Island (on the far side of Douglas Island), Whidby explored Taku Inlet. His passage was blocked by bergs. The basin at the end seemed sheathed in ice and the mountains wrapped in perpetual snow. He could find no place to land. Because of these negative early impressions and Auk Tlingit threats, it took nearly a century for newcomers to establish a foothold here.

Gold Creek, which winds its chilly course through downtown Juneau, was once a Tlingit fishing-camp site. The Tlingit called the creek *Dzantik'i Heeni,* or "where the flounder/flatfish gather." In autumn 1880 a local Aak'w (or Auk) Tlingit chief, Kowee, led two Canadian prospectors to the creek mouth. Kowee

Prospectors drawn by Juneau's gold strike, early 20th century.

TRACING JUNEAU'S GOLD BELT

Juneau's Gold Belt is an ore-rich corridor stretching from Dupont to Eagle River. With the help of wooden footbridges, gravel trails, and the occasional cable set into the rock face, you can trace the paths of miners all along this corridor.

One of the most accessible remnants of Juneau's mining past is **Basin Road.** You can reach it from the top of Gold Street; it hugs the lower slopes of Mt. Roberts. Walking this road, keep an ear peeled for the rush of Gold Creek in its canyon below, and catch glimpses of it from the massive wooden trestle bridge that leads into Last Chance Basin and Silver Bow Basin—the sites of Joe Juneau and Dick Harris's gold discoveries in 1880.

About a mile along Basin Road stands the **Last Chance Mining Museum,** clinging to the slope of Last Chance Basin (*see* Brief Excursions). This area once held a boarding house, bunkhouses, machine shops, and train sheds. Five hundred men labored in three shifts on the fifteen levels of Mt. Roberts during the peak years of activity (1915–35). Tunnels through the mountain connected this spot to the mill where the ore was processed; the skeleton of the mill can be seen on the slopes above downtown Juneau.

Just above the parking lot for the mining museum, at the first curve of **Perseverance Trail,** stands a shaft entrance. If you step into the entry you'll feel a blast of subterranean cold from the blocked tunnel. Imagine laboring in this ice box for eight hours at a stretch. The hike up Perseverance Trail, following the route of an old wagon road, is an easy climb. The trail is popular with joggers, but note that it is disintegrating on the downhill side.

For hikers unwilling to attempt Perseverance, **the flume** offers a more level walk. Accessed from a small parking lot at the end of Evergreen Avenue, the flume is a mile-long, boxed water trough. Once the flume carried water to create power for mining; today it carries part of the city's drinking water. Handrails and planking atop the wooden trough act as a boardwalk from the end of Evergreen Avenue to the first bridge on Basin Road. This elevated perch offers good views of rock slides and glimpses into the spruce and hemlock forest. Goat's beard, currants, stinging nettles, and the thorny devil's club flourish along the flume.

For another view of mining history, seek out the **Treadwell Historic Trail** on Douglas Island (*see* the Treadwell Past and Present sidebar).

was anxious to earn a reward offered by a Sitka mining engineer: 100 wool blankets plus day labor for his tribe. The prospectors, Joe Juneau and Richard Harris, frittered away their time on their first trip. However, on a second trip that year Kowee guided them up the creek into a high plateau called Bear's Nest (now Silver Bow Basin). The pair was ecstatic to find "large pieces of quartz spangled over with gold . . . little lumps as large as peas and beans." News of the strike spread quickly, and by the close of the year 30 miners were in residence. At first the town was called Harrisburgh, then Rockwell, and finally Juneau City—after Joe reputedly bought several rounds of drinks. By the following winter Juneau had a blacksmith shop, 150 miners, and 450 Tlingits.

Juneau forms the "buckle" of a mineralized district known as the Juneau Gold Belt. This district extends from Windham Bay north to the head of Lynn Canal,

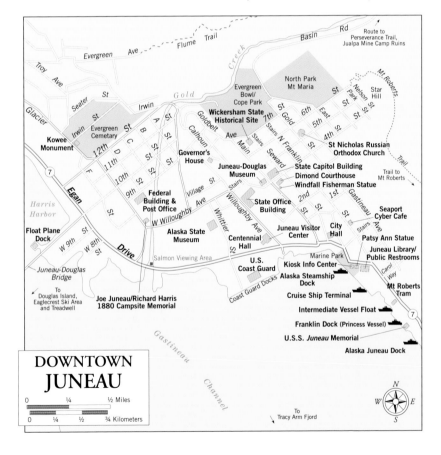

THE AMALGAM THIEVES

At the Treadwell mines, gold was crushed from the ore in the stamps. This gold was amalgamated with mercury in the stamp block. The gold-laden mercury, called amalgam, was then heated, causing the mercury to vaporize and leave pure gold. For several years prior to 1905, Supt. Kinzie had been disturbed because of a discrepancy between assay values or ore going into the mill and the gold recovered in the clean-ups. The assays consistently indicated that more gold should have been recovered.

Kinzie had hired the "cleverest Pinkerton detective in the west" who quickly noticed that Mrs. Mary Freestone made regular trips to Seattle. He followed her on one trip, and, in Seattle Mrs. Freestone went directly to an assay office where she deposited a retort full of gold under the name of C. T. Arthur.

The detective promptly had Mrs. Freestone arrested. The shock of the arrest "nearly prostrated" the woman and she confessed completely. It seemed that her husband would steal small portions of the amalgam, take it home and retort it there.

Mr. Freestone was arrested, and, when told of his wife's confession, broke down and freely admitted his crime. What had started as a small theft continued until a substantial amount of amalgam had been taken, from which about $3,400 of gold was retrieved by the Freestones.

—Earl Redman, *History of the Mines and Miners in the Juneau Gold Belt,* 1988.

about 120 miles total. A Geological Survey bulletin of 1906 notes, "In whatever direction one travels from Juneau within this belt, quartz mines are to be found in every stage, from the prospect to the highly developed mines." Gold mining held steady until World War II. Juneau was known for its mining innovations. As Juneau historian David Stone, author of *Hard Rock Gold,* recounts, the mines offered stock options, eight-hour shifts, and workmen's comp before these benefits were implemented anywhere else in the world.

From the 1830s on, Tlingit populations were devastated by a series of epidemics. Most surviving Natives lost faith in their traditions and sought Western schooling and religion. Meanwhile, tourists judged the area safe for travel. They visited mines, haggled for baskets, and returned home with gold-nugget watch

The Lynn Canal, one of the gateways to Juneau.

chains galore. Taku Glacier, which had discouraged Whidby, became a popular pause on cruise routes. As a result, steamships began delivering tourists to Juneau's Steamship Dock (now the Cruise Ship Terminal Dock) in 1884. Early sightseers interested in mining sought out the Treadwell properties on Douglas Island.

In 1906 the capital of Alaska was transferred from Sitka to Juneau, partially because Juneau's economic star was rising. The contrast between Sitka and Juneau is perhaps best expressed by Hannah Breece, who taught school in Alaska between 1904 and 1918. She passed through both ports in the summer of 1912 on her way to a teaching post at Fort Yukon. She found Sitka charming and quaint, "like a dear and proper old lady dozing in her chair. Juneau was like a strapping young fellow striding to his work."

The economy of Southeast Alaska has been described as a "three-legged stool" of fisheries, pulp mills, and tourism. As the state capital, Juneau has a fourth leg: the state legislature, whose 90-day sessions begin in January. Since the 1970s, voters in Anchorage have lobbied to move the capital closer to their doorstep, since half of Alaska's population now resides in or near Anchorage.

JUNEAU NOW *map pages 85 and 88*

Visitors may pigeonhole Juneau as a jumping-off spot for magnificence like Glacier Bay, 50 miles to the northwest. But Juneau is a destination in its own right. Just blocks above downtown lies a quaint historic district of Queen Anne–style homes and tiny miners' shacks. A dozen miles away the Mendenhall Valley presents quiet, tree-lined residential streets resembling exterior shots from *Father Knows Best*. Juneau revolves around several hubs, including the waterfront and business district; the headquarters of the 17th Coast Guard on Egan Drive; residences and schools near 12th Street; a handful of small boat harbors; "the Valley"; and the University of Alaska Southeast. Each area has its fan club.

There's a saying in the Last Frontier that its cities are "only 20 minutes from Alaska." In other words, untouched wilderness thrives a short distance from the busiest thoroughfare. This juxtaposition is particularly striking in Juneau, where black bears amble through perennial beds so often that black-oil sunflower seeds in bird feeders are discouraged.

Walk toward Mount Juneau from downtown in June and you'll soon hear a low thrumming issuing from the forested slopes. It's the mating song of the male blue grouse. Crows kibitz from the branches of mountain ash, making sounds like

LIGHTHOUSES

A dozen lighthouses stand guard on or near the dangerous rocks and reefs of the Inside Passage. Needed for safe navigation in the passage's tricky waters, especially in dense fog or whiteout conditions, their lights warn ships to steer clear of hazards.

As you sail north, the lighthouses along the route include Tree Point at Dixon Entrance; Mary Island in Revillagigedo Channel; Cape Decision on Sumner Strait; Five Fingers in Stephens Passage; Point Retreat, Sentinel Island, and Eldred Rock in Lynn Canal near Juneau; and Cape Spencer in Cross Sound.

These lighthouses were once manned by keepers who filled the lamps with seal or whale oil and polished the big lenses that helped magnify the light. Today, however, all lights are fully automated, powered by solar batteries. Some are being restored by local historical societies; some can be rented. Informational plaques along Steamship Dock Wharf explain the history of Alaska's lighthouses.

In addition to lighthouses, the Inside Passage has navigational aids such as red and green buoys, lighted buoys, and blinking signals. Signs on shore warn of underwater cables or other hazards. Wrangell Narrows is so dangerous that more than 70 navigational markers guide ships along the 21 miles between Wrangell and Petersburg--there are so many lights that Alaskans have nicknamed this passage "Christmas Tree Lane."

rakes on concrete. Occasionally they imitate cats. The "ringing telephone" is the varied thrush—a black and orange songster slightly larger than a robin.

North of town, the Mendenhall is Juneau's "drive-up" glacier. The Mendenhall is retreating, meaning it melts faster at its snout or terminus than it grows at its source. The Taku Glacier is advancing, with more ice added by snowfall at its source than it loses from melting. Both are part of the Juneau Ice Field, as are the Herbert and Eagle glaciers "out the road." (Juneau's "road system" is minor arteries plus a 20-mile-long highway headed north. Anything along the highway is called "out the road.") South of town, Taku Glacier is a popular site, but cannot be accessed by road.

The status of gold mining as an aspect of Juneau's history may be about to change. Juneau's three largest hard-rock gold mines, the Treadwell Complex, the Alaska Gastineau, and the Alaska-Juneau or A-J, produced seven million ounces of gold while they were in operation in the early 20th century. With the price of gold rising in recent years—those seven million ounces would be worth about $3 billion in 2004 values—new mining ventures are under consideration.

WALKING TOURS

Juneau offers so much to see that a single walking tour is insufficient. Below, I've broken up sightseeing walks by themes. Each of these walks will take one to two hours.

HISTORIC DOWNTOWN JUNEAU

Many of the original buildings built in the 1880s and 1890s still stand. Within a seven-block radius there are 60 buildings built before 1904. Eleven are listed on the National Register of Historic Places; just a few are open to the public. Some, like the Alaska Steam Laundry (174 South Franklin; 1901, now a mall) are not particularly impressive, but others are definitely eye-catching.

Start at the three-story **Alaskan Hotel & Bar** (167 South Franklin; 907/586–1000). This is Juneau's oldest continuously operating hostelry. When the Alaskan's doors opened on September 16, 1913, Champagne flowed, two bands played, and free ferries brought guests over from Douglas. The hotel was cutting-edge at the time, because it featured steam heat and a wireless station of 1.5 kilowatts on the roof. A window flanking the front door retains its Tiffany stained glass. Owners Mike and Bettye Adams furnished the 30 guest rooms with antique oak, and they had the basement outfitted with a bar, grill, and dance floor.

Next, turn right and continue up South Franklin. At 229 North Franklin, take in the 1904 **William Winn/Bell House.** Its style is "Juneau eclectic," meaning it began as a no-nonsense residence/boardinghouse but took on airs in 1986 when Queen Anne gingerbread and "painted lady" hues were added. Robert Stroud, the pimp who became famous as "the Birdman of Alcatraz," is said to have boarded here. The house is just a block and a half from the spot where, in 1909, Stroud violently murdered a bartender he thought had cheated him.

Make a detour left on Fourth Street to visit the **Alaska State Capitol** (Seward and Fourth Sts.; 907/465–2479). On summer weekdays you can take a free guided tour. The pillared building (1929–31) is used by the legislature January through March.

Continue uphill, taking a right on Fifth. The ★St. Nicholas Russian Orthodox Church (326 Fifth St.; 907/586-6790) has a dramatic setting, with the rock-slide scars and dark forest of Mt. Juneau rising behind it. The church (1897) is the oldest unaltered church in Southeast Alaska. It was either constructed on site—or built in Russia, disassembled, and shipped here. No one is quite sure. But its octagonal shape and gold onion dome make it a favorite with photographers and painters. The interior is a gilded jewel box of icons and artwork, some dating from the 18th century. You're welcome to attend an incense-scented service, held in the church language of Slavic, but custom dictates one stands throughout. The bookstore/gift shop adjoining is even larger than the church.

From the church, ascend Gold Street to Sixth, then hang a left. Pause on the left-hand sidewalk to take in **The Family,** a three-part totem carved by local artist Michael Beasley in 1996. Next, take a right onto the second staircase you come to. Tucked into the corner formed by this staircase and Sixth Street is the J.M. Davis House, the residence of Frances Brooks, a British painter who moved to Juneau in 1891, and J. Montgomery Davis, whom she married in 1892. As you climb, there are clear views of its gardens of foxgloves, daisies, primroses, columbine, and rugosa roses, as well as glimpses into other colorful, terraced plots. At the top is Chicken Ridge—named for the ptarmigan that early miners bagged here. To your right stands the **Hammond-Wickersham House** (213 Seventh St.; 907/586–9001), a mansion built in 1899 for the superintendent of the Sheep Creek Mine. Its most famous resident was Judge James Wickersham, politician and author, who bought the house in 1928. This house is occasionally open; call for availability. To see the judge's view from his glassed-in porch, walk onto the lawn and turn toward the Channel.

From the Wickersham House, turn left on Seventh Street. Pause at its intersection with Main Street for a San Francisco–like view down the steep street to the steamship wharf. If you descend Main for three blocks, you're back at the State Capitol and the City Museum.

ANIMALS

For a great photo op, climb on the **Windfall Fisherman** on Seward Street in front of the Dimond Courthouse. The life-size bronze of a grizzly content with his catch was designed by R. T. Wallen, a sculptor who knows his bear anatomy well. Juneau's most famous animal statue is **Patsy Ann,** posed alertly on the

A snowy day in downtown Juneau.

steamship wharf at Marine Park. Patsy Ann (1929–42) was a deaf bull terrier who "heard" the whistles of approaching ships and faithfully met vessels as they tied up at this wharf. Observe animals of another kind at the downtown hangouts on Front Street, like the Viking Bar and the Imperial.

TOTEM POLES AND LOCAL ARTIFACTS

Juneau's **totem poles** may not be tidily grouped together in a park, but they're well worth seeking out. There were 20 poles at last count. Downtown examples include Amos Wallace's Harnessing the Atom Totem near the City Museum on Calhoun Street. The venerable Waasgo or Old Witch Pole, in the lobby of the State Office Building at Fourth and Calhoun streets, was carved by Dwight Wallace in 1880 for the Quit-aas clan at Sukwan. Old Witch was originally moved to Juneau to lure customers to a souvenir shop, then moved indoors in 1977. Almost no poles of this vintage remain in existence, so the Old Witch is a rare bird indeed. Juneau's newest totem is a sinuous, unpainted pole in the foyer of the Mt. Roberts Tramway at the cruise-ship dock.

Pore over the relief map of Juneau in 1967 at the **Juneau-Douglas City Museum** (Fourth and Main Sts.; 907/586-3572). The detailed map was created by a high school student using aerial photos and contour maps, to a scale of 1 inch to 1,320 feet (or 4 inches to the mile). A pull-out step helps kids get a good look. Another draw is the remains of a basketry fish trap excavated from Montana Creek in 1991. The trap is about 700 years old and has a full-size model suspended above it, plus hands-on supplemental materials. Mineral core samples,

ROOTS TRAVEL: FINDING GREAT-GRANDDAD

Are you looking for Great Granddad, the mysterious missing miner? If so, you'll find excellent resources in the Inside Passage. Some of the 100,000 stampeders who headed for Alaska and the Yukon during the Klondike Gold Rush traveled under assumed names. Some disappeared. Others hunkered down at remote creeks and never wrote home. But if there are any traces of them, you have a good shot of finding them here.

Cemeteries might give you a lead, such as the Gold Rush Cemetery in Skagway. Most graves there date from 1898 to 1904.

Instead of reading headstones, you could search through turn-of-the-20th-century documents. Visit the **Skagway Museum & Archive** (Seventh and Spring Sts. P. O. Box 521, Skagway 99804; 907/983–2420). The Archive keeps records of persons crossing the Canadian border during the Stampede years, plus additional details from logs kept by the Royal Canadian Mounted Police. The archive also houses passenger lists from the White Pass Steamship Line and Skagway and Dawson prison files.

The **Juneau-Douglas City Museum** (Fourth and Main Sts.; 907/586–3572) is a treasure trove for amateur genealogists. "Many prospectors looking for gold in Alaska came through Juneau," notes Ellen Carrlee, Curator of Collections. "If relatives have a range of years when they suspect an ancestor was here, that's helpful. A full name with middle initial and names of partners or wives are also useful in tracing people. There are lots of places where people had to register. If they collected Social Security here, or ran for office, those records may show birth date, death date, and place of death." The museum has an index of employees of the Alaska-Juneau Mine (1897–44) and its shop sells copies of historical studies and limited-edition references.

The **Alaska State Library** in Juneau has prepared an "Alaska Genealogy Resource Guide," copies of which can be found on its Web site, www.library.state.ak.us.

The Alaska State Archives, located downstairs from the Alaska State Library at 141 Willoughby Street, stores probate documents and court records (907/465–2270; www.archives.state.ak.us/).

For Internet research, try the **Yukon & Alaska Genealogy Centre** in Whitehorse site, www.yukonalaska.com/pathfinder/gen/, which allows access to information assembled by Pathfinder Publications and others. Sample databases include an index to proprietors and managers of historic Alaska and Yukon hotels, saloons, and cafés, and a list of the 203 families in the Matanuska Colony.

A CMT (culturally modified tree) on Mt. Roberts.

prospectors' shopping lists, a dugout canoe and period "rooms" in glass cases are favorites in the permanent exhibit.

THE GOVERNOR'S HOUSE AND THE WATERFRONT

Tailings (waste rock) from the Alaska-Juneau Mine were laid down to create much of Juneau's modern waterfront, including the flat land where Egan Drive now stretches. The original waterfront followed Willoughby to Front Street and around to South Franklin. The 1896 Lewis Building (now McDonald's at 130 Front St.) was one of the first claimed lots in town and once stood at the water's edge at high tide.

To tour this area, begin at the **Governor's House** (716 Calhoun St.), an uphill walk from downtown. The white clapboard residence (1912) has been termed "a liberal interpretation of New England colonial" architecture. It's not open to visitors except on rare occasions, such as an afternoon in December when thousands of cookies baked by the Governor's chef are gobbled by locals.

Flanking the front door of the Governor's House is a yellow-cedar totem carved by Charlie Tagook and William Brown of Klukwan and Saxman in 1939–40. Although known as the ★**Mosquito Legend pole**, this pole incorporates symbols of several Raven legends. The top two figures are Raven and

Several historic buildings cluster on or near Franklin Street.

Grandfather Raven, or Nass Shagi Yeil, "Chief at the head of Nass River." They recall the story of an earth in total darkness. Raven learned that Nass Shagi Yeil kept three cedar boxes in which he stored sources of light: the sun, moon, and stars. Raven journeyed to the head of Nass, transformed himself into a spruce needle, and was swallowed with a drink of water by Nass's daughter. The evergreen needle made her pregnant, and Raven was soon born as a human child. The spoiled grandson cried for his grandfather's prized boxes as playthings, and liberated the sun, moon, and stars.

Another figure shows Haayee Shaanak'w or "Old Woman Underneath"—a spirit said to hold up the world on the foreleg of a beaver. One day, very hungry, Raven went to Old Woman Underneath and asked her to lower the ocean to make it easier for him to gather sea urchins to eat. At first she refused, but when Raven threatened her, she created a shallow ocean. Since then, the world's oceans have risen and fallen twice a day.

The figure with the long beak is Mosquito. Above him is Guteel, a bogeyman figure. In prehistoric times, when hunters failed to return home Guteel was said to have eaten them. Eventually men decided to capture Guteel. They succeeded in luring him into a pit and setting him on fire, but as he approached his end, Guteel declared, "Even though you kill me, I will continue to bite you." His ashes flew into the air as innumerable mosquitoes.

Turn back toward downtown and look for a wooden overpass bearing a yellow sign, "13 ft. 7 in." Just before this overpass is a staircase heading down, down, down. (There's a bench on one landing.) Descend to Willoughby Avenue and you're at the site of the Aak'w Village. This was a summer fish camp until 1883, when Kowee and others moved here permanently to be nearer the cash economy. The beach line at that time followed where Willoughby is today.

Once on Willoughby Avenue, you'll be within easy reach of the ★Alaska State Museum (395 Whittier St.; 907/465–2901). To bone up on local history and culture, follow the curve of Willoughby to your right, then turn left onto Whittier. You'll see the parklike setting of the museum one block ahead. The permanent exhibits focus on Alaska's Native peoples, Russian America, and the land's history after the American purchase. You'll see mementos such as bricks of tea used in early trade and gleaming Russian samovars. The gift shop here is worth browsing for books and Native arts.

If you're skipping the museum, simply follow Willoughby to its intersection with Gold Creek. Just over the bridge stands a **monument to Harris and Juneau,** marking the site of their original camp. If you head along the creek for

KID STUFF

- The **Alaska State Museum** hands out a free Kids' Guide to maps and Native culture exhibits. The guide's word games, riddles, and puzzles help explain the cultures of Eskimos, Aleuts, and Northwest Coast Indians. Don't miss the eagle tree diorama; ascend a spiral ramp to see it from all sides. At the top of the ramp, visit the children's gallery for a little dress-up or board a partial, one-third-scale model of Capt. Vancouver's ship *Discovery*.

- Follow your nose to the **Alaskan Fudge Company** (195 South Franklin St.; 907/586–1478) where you can watch chocolates being dipped by hand and fudge tempered on marble slabs.

- Try your luck from the public fishing dock next to the **Macaulay Hatchery** (2697 Channel Dr., 3 miles from downtown). Remember, small fish can put up a big fight, so wear a life jacket.

about a block, it intersects with Egan Drive. From the bridges here, spawning salmon can be seen milling about in late August.

BRIEF EXCURSIONS

Get a lift from the **Mount Roberts Tramway** (907/463–3412). The tramway's base is near the cruise-ship docks; in six minutes you'll ride up 1,800 feet to an observatory complex, which includes a live bald eagle, the Timberline Bar & Grill, a theater, and a nature center. Marmots sometimes scurry about near the nature center. Check out the free film, *Seeing Daylight*, which gives a glimpse of Native culture from the Tlingit point of view. Native artists sometimes give demonstrations, or you might catch a tale from a Native storyteller. Fit hikers can descend the Mount Roberts Trail in under an hour and a half, but keep in mind that it's steep and has switchbacks––some with dramatic dropoffs. When purchasing a ticket for the Mt. Roberts Tram, consider their **Dungeness crab feed,** available mid-June to mid-August. The crab is caught near Icy Strait and delivered live for the all-you-can-eat dinner ($29.95), which includes appetizers and salads. And you can watch crab swimming in a live tank near the dining area.

Practice your Tarzan yawp on a **zipline tour.** Alaska Canopy Adventures (907/225–5503) will fly you over the glory hole on Douglas Island. Allow 2 or 3 hours. Alaska Zipline Adventures (3000 Fish Creek Rd.; 907/321–0947) whisks you through the treetops. Allow 4 hours.

For a chance to do some cooking of your own, sign up for a 50-minute culinary experience with Laraine Derr's **Chez Alaska Cooking School** (907/790–2639). The school uses the facilities of the Alaska Seafood Marketing Institute at 311 North Franklin Street, just a couple of blocks from downtown's shopping district. Demonstration classes are available daily and include a glass of wine and a recipe. Derr catches the salmon herself, and also may cook with fresh halibut, shrimp, black cod, or crab.

Take in the **Taku Fisheries Ice House** (alley off South Franklin St.; no phone) on the sea side of the Twisted Fish Grill. Although from January through March Juneau appears to be a gabble of legislators and from May through September a gaggle of T-shirt vendors, it is a working fishing port. View the action first-hand at the Ice House. Fishing vessels anchor below the dock; their catches are unloaded at the top. The fish are either lifted in cargo nets, raised in totes (large plastic boxes), or whisked up through a tube resembling a giant dryer exhaust. Everything from halibut to gleaming silvers to bright orange rock fish is sorted here in season. Then saunter around the Grill to Taku's retail shop to sample smoked salmon.

Board a bus or taxi for the 12-mile ride to the ★Mendenhall Glacier (Glacier Spur Rd.; 907/789–0097). Mendenhall's drive-up accessibility makes it one of the world's most-visited glaciers, with over 300,000 sightseers a year. Along the easy switchback path to its visitors center (wheelchair accessible; $3 fee), you can see grooves etched in the rock by moving ice. Inside the center, floor-to-ceiling windows open onto excellent views of Mendenhall Lake, which lies between the center and the glacier itself, and Photo Point Overlook. The lake is often dotted with small icebergs calved from the glacier's snout; the glacier itself is blue and white, streaked with brown. Peer through the telescopes on hand and you might spot grazing mountain goats. Photo Point Overlook, as the name suggests, is a favorite posing spot; locals often use Mendenhall as a backdrop for wedding photos. The center has a handful of displays on glaciers, including a relief map of the ice field and guides to such terms as crevasse, moraine, cirque, and plant succession. A short film on Mendenhall Glacier plays every 15 minutes in a comfortable theater. Kid-friendly exhibits include a swatch of mountain-goat fleece and a sample of rock flour (glacial silt).

MENDENHALL GLACIER

Seattle has its drive-up espresso stands, Las Vegas drive-up wedding chapels, and California . . . well, California may have a drive-up for just about anything, but none have Alaska's drive-up glaciers. Mendenhall Glacier is one of more than thirty glaciers that squeeze like toothpaste from the 1,500-square-mile Juneau Ice Field . . . . Each year 300,000 people visit this river of ice by bus or car and hundreds more on foot, bikes, roller skates, and cross-country ski in winter.

Yet with each passing year, Mendenhall becomes less approachable. Until 1750 the glacier was advancing, its face nearly two and a half miles closer to where Juneau was to be settled in the nineteenth century. Since then the glacier has retreated steadily—nearly three hundred feet in 2000 alone. In all the face has pulled back nearly a half mile from where it was when the visitor center was built in 1962. At some point in the not so distant future, the visitor center may have to be moved just to keep the glacier in view.

—Harry M. Walker, *Wacky & Wonderful Roadside Attractions of Alaska,* 2002.

For a unique view of Mendenhall Glacier, sign up for a kayaking trip in Gastineau Channel.

The rocky promontory on which the visitors center was built was once within arm's reach of the ice. In 1935 you could stand there and touch the face of the glacier—but since then the glacier has retreated a mile and a half to its current length of 12 miles long. (It's over a mile wide.) Mendenhall has been receding for over 200 years. Between 1980 and 2000 its average loss was 90 feet a year. In 2004, however, it surprised the U.S. Forest Service by receding 600 feet—leading USFS to begin using the term "global warming." As the glacier retreats, it exposes bare rock that is gradually able to support vegetation. On your way to the visitors center, for instance, you'll pass cottonwoods, willows, and alder growing in shallow pockets of soil that have accumulated during the past century. Allow two hours for this excursion, not including the drive.

To stretch your legs, walk the easy 1½-mile **Moraine Ecology Trail,** or the half-mile Trail of Time. Or try the quarter-mile Photo Point Trail, which leads onto a peninsula of glacier-grooved and polished boulders, giving you good views of the glacier face and thundering Nugget Falls. A massive rock slide in 2005 made hiking out to the Falls, a round-trip of about a mile, more difficult. As you move closer to the face, it's like stepping into a cold-storage facility. However, be careful not to disturb terns (small white birds) nesting on grass or sand on the flats around the lake.

Hundreds of miles of mining tunnels honeycomb Mount Roberts, but most are sealed off. One company, however, can get you in. Princess Tours (907/463–3900; www.princess.com) leads Juneau's only **underground mining tour** with A-J Mine/Gastineau Mill Enterprises. A van takes you to the ore-crushing plant and conveyer tunnel. Guides explain how stamps (rock crushers) work and how the ore traveled from mine shaft to rock crusher. Walk into a mine shaft of what was once the world's largest producing gold mine and watch experienced miners demonstrate their noisy craft. (Hard hats and ear plugs are provided.) The tour takes about three hours.

For more mining memorabilia, visit the **Last Chance Mining Museum & Historical Park,** operated by the Gastineau Channel Historical Society (1001 Basin Rd.; 907/586–5338; $4). The museum occupies the restored compressor building (1912) of the Alaska-Juneau Mine, listed on the National Register of Historic Places. It's chockablock with machinery. The original compressor, which has a 750 horsepower motor, is not fired up because it would be deafening, but a Gade engine is occasionally started, going "chugga, chugga, pooh!" Be sure to check out the mock tunnel with tools and equipment. On the grounds are unrestored locomotives and passenger cars. Stroll from downtown to the end of Gold

Street, then along scenic Basin Road for about three-quarters of a mile to the mine, reached via a footbridge. Basin Road provides excellent views across Gold Creek to Mount Juneau, where slide areas are evident and mountain goats can sometimes be seen grazing. Plan on at least two hours for the walk and visit.

Neophyte paddlers may head to the North Douglas boat ramp for a **guided kayak trip** in the direction of Mendenhall Glacier. Alaska Travel Adventures offers this excursion (907/789–0052) in two-person kayaks, with escorts in motorized skiffs. The tour includes instruction, gear, and a light snack. Of the 3½ hours involved, about 2 are spent paddling.

The Juneau Parks and Recreation Department sponsors **guided hikes** (907/586–0428; www.juneau.org/parkrec/hike) on Wednesday and Saturday year-round. This is a good opportunity to meet locals and quiz them at length. For information about hiking trails, see the Trail Mix Web site, www.juneau trails.org.

Glacier Gardens Rainforest Adventure (7600 Glacier Highway, about 7 miles north of downtown; 907/790–3377) is a window into the Tongass National Forest that's a good choice primarily for travelers with mobility problems. This botanical garden shows what ingenuity and "sweat equity" can accomplish with a seemingly useless welter of mud. Owners Cindy and Steve Bowhay started their park in 1994 with seven acres of land ravaged by a landslide. Tree trunks and rocks were flung everywhere. The Bowhays channeled a meandering creek into ponds and repurposed uprooted trees. Steve imaginatively "planted" the fallen trees upside down to create "flower towers," using their flat root structures to grow petunias, fuchsias, and begonias in the sky.

The garden now encompasses 50 acres, including an eight-foot-wide golf-cart path to a boardwalk outlook. From this lookout point you'll have a panoramic view of the Mendenhall Wetlands, the shallows of Gastineau Channel, and the Lynn Canal. Golf-cart tours wind through a landscaped hillside area and up into uncultivated rain forest. Guides discuss the flora, and you might spot a river otter, an eagle, a falcon, or even a bear. Allow an hour to two hours for this tour. Visitors can stroll through the street-level gardens and greenhouses on their own, but an entrance fee is charged.

Head over to rocky Mayflower Island to see the **John Rishel Mineral Information Center** (907/364–1551), a lesser-known museum but a treasure

(following pages) Ice meets ocean at the Tracy Arm Fjord, one of the world's most dramatic fjords.

Distin Lake within Admiralty
Island National Monument.

trove for fans of geodes and quartz crystals. The ground floor houses the Tom Pittman Geology and Mining Museum, stuffed with displays of hundreds of Alaska's minerals, from fool's gold to the real thing, as well as rock and fossil specimens. Historic photos and artifacts illustrate Juneau's gold-mining era. The center can easily be reached by public transportation or by car from downtown Juneau. (A short causeway connects Mayflower Island to Douglas.) Allow at least an hour for the trip.

LONGER OUTINGS

One of the most popular day trips from Juneau is a boat trip to ★Tracy Arm Fjord. Thirty miles long, Tracy Arm is considered one of the world's most dramatic fjords. Tucked away in a corner of the Tongass National Forest, 40 miles south of Juneau, the narrow fjord twists and turns between granite heights. Some of these sheer cliffs climb 2,000 feet. During a cruise here you'll likely see waterfalls, seals resting on icebergs, and a bald eagle or two. At the head of the fjord you come face-to-face with the twin Sawyer Glaciers. Blue ice flows into the aquamarine ocean—the blue intensified if the day is overcast. When the snout of a Sawyer calves, you'll instantly grasp why the Tlingit name for one glacier was *Sumdum,* a rendering of the drum-roll noise of calving. A cruise here takes about 9½ hours. Goldbelt Tours (800/820–2628; www.goldbelttours.com) is one of the companies to visit Tracy Arm. Its package includes lunch and a naturalist talk on the fjord. Adventure Bound (907/463–2509) is another cruise company that offers visits to Tracy Arm with on-board naturalists.

Combine peeks at peaks with a seafood treat at a 1920s log lodge. **Wings Airways** (907/586–6275) organizes three-hour floatplane excursions departing from downtown Juneau. You'll see views of five glaciers, and end your trip with a king salmon dinner at a Taku Glacier Lodge.

If bear-watching tops your life list, make the effort to get out to **Pack Creek on Admiralty Island.** This island, on the far side of Douglas Island from Juneau, reputedly has the world's highest concentration of brown bears. At Pack Creek you can hike a mile to a viewing tower. If hiking through bear-infested territory makes your hair stand on end, set up shop on a spit where you can perch on a log, zero in with a telescope, and have a ranger at hand at all times. Peak season for observing brown bears noshing on salmon is July 5 to August 15. This is after the breeding season, and, since there is plenty of food, aggression between bears is limited. Pack Creek can be reached only by floatplane or boat. The Forest Service

TREADWELL PAST AND PRESENT

The easy, two-mile **Treadwell Historic Trail** on Douglas Island leads through the remains of what was once a richly productive hard-rock gold-mining operation. Lulled by the trail's dappled light and birdsong, it's a mental stretch to visualize or "hear" the booming Treadwell complex that sprang up here at the turn of the 20th century. John Treadwell, the developer, created a far-reaching operation that ultimately included four mines and an entire company town. Seventy million dollars' worth of ore was extracted between 1882 and 1917.

To reach the trailhead from downtown Juneau, head across the Douglas Bridge, turn left, and walk three miles to the end of the road. The trail begins behind the picnic shelters at Sandy Beach, where a stamp (pulverizing mill) has been rescued from another location. During the mines' best years, 1900–1910, 880 such stamps thundered up and down 96 times a minute, pounding constantly 363 days a year. Miners operated in three eight-hour shifts and celebrated only two holidays: Fourth of July and Christmas.

Hundreds of miners were drawn here from as far away as China, and by the early 1900s a busy company town was in place. The boardinghouse fed 500 miners at a seating, while the Treadwell Club offered billiards and a 2,000-volume library. Groceries were delivered to homes by a St. Bernard pulling a rumbling wagon along the boardwalk. A large swimming pool, the Natatorium, was built in 1910, with showers, lockers, and dressing rooms as well as a swimming instructor.

In early 1909 there were 1,900 men on the payroll. A central shaft was sunk to 2,817 feet in 1916. But as tunnels bored deeper and drove beneath Gastineau Channel, the land became unstable. The ground surface began actively moving on February 1, 1917. The end came on April 21–22, when a stream the size of "the Yukon at White Horse rapids" began flowing into the Natatorium and the fire hall. Soon the main ore pit, the Glory Hole, collapsed. Luckily, not a single miner died in the collapse, but with the bells of the hoisting signals silenced, most of the employees soon moved on.

Walking the trail, you'll pass the Glory Hole, an assay office, and a massive water tank still tied to the Treadwell Ditch (a deep trough that collected water from several creeks). The area is honeycombed with shafts and pits, so stay on the trail. Along the way, bits of tram track and a huge steel water tank can be glimpsed in the underbrush. At the end of the trail, cyanide and arsenic (used in the ore extraction) have left their mark—no plants grow.

Snapping the icebergs of Tracy Arm Fjord.

limits the daily number of visitors to 12, so take care to register in advance with the Admiralty Island National Monument office (907/586–8790). Flight services that access Pack Creek include Alaska Fly-N-Fish (907/790–2120), Alaska Seaplane Service (907/789–3331), and Wings of Alaska (907/789–9863). Save a day for this trip.

In September, Gastineau Channel Historical Society offers a once-a-year treat, the **Lighthouse Cruise & Keeper's Lunch** (907/586–5338). This six-hour cruise takes you to Sentinel Island, Eldred Rock, and Point Retreat lighthouses. Pause at Vanderbilt Reef for lunch, live music, and shipwreck/lighthouse history by members of the society.

FAVORITE PLACES TO SHOP

Downtown Juneau is stuffed to the gills with sources of off-color T-shirts, mugs, baby bibs bearing pink moose, shot glasses bearing brown moose, resin totems, Canadian jade, and the like. But there are also amber necklaces, Russian icons with silver overlays, prints on paper made from local plants, and hand-painted ostrich eggs.

Head for **Raven's Journey** (439 South Franklin St.; 907/463–48686) or **Hummingbird Hollow** (Juneau Airport; 907/789–4672) for traditional works in walrus ivory, whalebone, copper, and wood, as well as Native dolls and modern glass art. Raven's Journey also carries delectable Aleut, Eskimo, and Tlingit baskets. Tlingit artists Mick and Rick Beasley opened **Beasley's Art Gallery** (8853 N. Douglas Hwy., 907/586–3980) in 1999. They're known for their luscious pile rugs in totemic designs as well as frontlets, masks, prints, and jewelry. They work with authentic materials such as ermine skins and trade beads. It's easy to covet everything in the shop.

The **Mt. Juneau Trading Post** (151 South Franklin St.; 907/586–3426) smells like an old-fashioned trading post: of quills and caribou hides, bark, cedar, ancient bone—and tanning agents better left anonymous. This is the place for masks of all descriptions and dimensions, mammoth tusk jewelry, and the silver bracelets local ladies stack on their forearms. Take the stairs to browse carefully selected books.

FAVORITE PLACES TO EAT

Douglas Cafe. Just across the Gastineau Channel from downtown Juneau, Douglas Café serves up "Juneau's best" burgers at lunch. In the evening the lights dim and the cook dishes up chicken Marsala, apple-brandy pork, Cajun prawn fettucine, and fresh salmon. Photographs of Douglas Island in 1900 line the walls. *916 Third St., Douglas Island; 907/364–3307. Limited hours Oct.–Apr.* **$–$$**

Sandpiper Café. This sunny eatery two blocks from the State Museum serves breakfast and lunch only, closing at 2 PM daily. Breakfast dishes include a French toast and pancakes. For lunch, try a veal, elk, or venison burger. For something to nosh aboard ship or in your hotel room, consider the bakery's scones. *429 West Willoughby Ave.; 907/586–3150.* **$–$$**

Thane Ore House Salmon Bake. Make the trek to this beachfront spot for all-you-can-eat alder-grilled king or sockeye salmon, beer-battered halibut, and barbecued beef ribs. The space is decorated with mining memorabilia. There's a shuttle available from downtown Juneau. *4400 Thane Rd; 907/586–3442. Closed Sept.–Apr.* **$–$$**

Zen. An Asian fusion menu means your fresh halibut might be dolloped with ginger-infused sauce, and your black cod may be accompanied by stir-fried veggies. Breakfast, served until 2 PM Monday through Saturday, is all-American, with fresh-baked cinnamon rolls and biscuits. Sunday brings an all-you-can-eat brunch. *Goldbelt Hotel, 51 Egan Dr.; 907/586–5075.* **$$–$$$**

S K A G W A Y

Compact, breezy Skagway beckons from a northern finger of the Inside Passage. This seaport sits on a deep-water fjord, Taiya Inlet, at the head of Lynn Canal—a lovely 90-mile journey from Juneau between banks that seem untouched by human hands. When Klondike stampeder and budding author Jack London came here in 1897, he traveled in a Tlingit freight canoe. Oddly enough, London didn't describe this trip in any of the dozens of stories rooted in his northern adventures; perhaps it was simply too peaceful.

In prehistoric times, Skagway was a trailhead—a place for hauling the dugout ashore and continuing on foot. Settlement here began in historic times as a lone cabin nestled on the delta fan of the Skagway River. The delta spills from a canyon, embraced on three sides by steep wooded slopes. Until 1970 Skagway lacked a road connection to the outside world. It could be reached only by railroad, ferry, and small aircraft. Today a well-maintained road leads to Carcross and Whitehorse, Yukon Territory, where it connects with the Alaska-Canada or Al-Can Highway. Tourism is now the town's main industry, with the cruise ships docking from the first week in May through September. Many visitors take to "the longest museum in the world"—the Chilkoot Pass Trail—while others simply walk Broadway, imagining the town in its gold-rush heyday.

SKAGWAY THEN

The original Skagway settler was crusty, loquacious Captain William "Billy" Moore, a former riverboat pilot. He and a Tlingit companion, Skookum Jim, hiked over the 45-mile White Pass route early in 1887 and thought it would do well as a route to the interior. Moore consequently staked claim to 160 acres on the delta fan of the Skagway River, built a log cabin, and became the area's first white settler. In the fall of 1887 he and his son Ben broke the silence by hammering together a wharf.

The settlement might have remained inconsequential but for an 1896 gold strike near Dawson City in the Klondike. When dozens of successful miners disembarked at major West Coast ports toting fortunes in gold nuggets and dust in July 1897, Americans were wrestling with a major economic depression. The dream of easy riches drew tens of thousands north—most of them to the sister

The White Pass & Yukon Route Railway steams through the mountains.

FAQS

Who was Captain Moore?

Captain William Moore was a tough cuss with a nose for settlement patterns. The former riverboat captain was rugged enough to secure the first contract to deliver mail in the Yukon in 1896—at age 74. He is sometimes called the "discoverer" of the White Pass Trail. (It had been used for centuries by Tlingit traders.) Moore's claim to fame is twofold. First, he believed that gold would be discovered in the Yukon Valley. Second, he guessed that the White Pass Trail would be important for access to the Yukon. Moore put his stamp on his theories by staking claim to 160 acres on Skagway Bay and becoming its first Caucasian settler in 1887, ten years before George Carmack's bonanza gold discovery became common knowledge.

What does "skookum" mean?

Skookum is a term in the Chinook trading language meaning "strong," "big," or "replete with rapids." Chinook was a basic, 250-word vocabulary used by voyageurs, prospectors, and Hudson's Bay traders for common terms like "food" and "bear." It was created by simplifying Chinook Indian words and combining them with scraps of other Native American words as well as French and English terms. Adventurer–authors like John Muir and Jack London picked up bits of this trading jargon and larded their prose with it to add local flavor.

What is the origin of the name Skagway?

This place name derives from the Tlingit term meaning "place where the north wind blows" or "home of the north wind." In other words, hold onto your hat!

Follow the tracks of gold miners with a trip on the White Pass & Yukon Route Railroad.

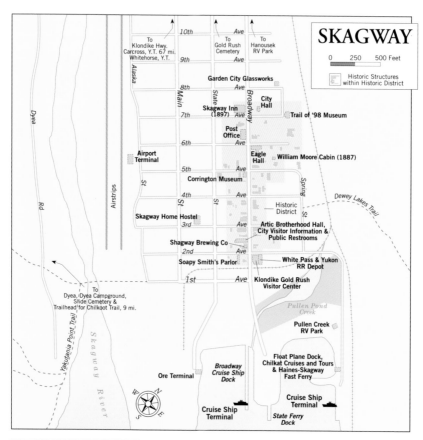

SKAGWAY

0   250   500 Feet

[ ] Historic Structures within Historic District

10th Ave
To Klondike Hwy. Carcross, Y.T. 67 mi. Whitehorse, Y.T.
To Gold Rush Cemetery
To Hanousek RV Park
9th Ave

Garden City Glassworks
8th Ave

City Hall
Skagway Inn (1897)
7th Ave
Trail of '98 Museum

Post Office
6th Ave

Airport Terminal

Eagle Hall
William Moore Cabin (1887)
5th Ave

Corrington Museum
4th Ave

Historic District

Skagway Home Hostel
3rd Ave

Artic Brotherhood Hall, City Visitor Information & Public Restrooms

Shagway Brewing Co
2nd Ave

Soapy Smith's Parlor

White Pass & Yukon RR Depot

1st Ave

Klondike Gold Rush Visitor Center

To Dyea, Dyea Campground, Slide Cemetery & Trailhead for Chilkoot Trail, 9 mi.

Pullen Pond Creek

Pullen Creek RV Park

Dyea Rd

Airstrips

Alaska

Main St

State St

Broadway

Spring St

Dewey Lakes Trail

Yakutania Point Trail

Skagway River

Float Plane Dock, Chilkat Cruises and Tours & Haines-Skagway Fast Ferry

Ore Terminal
Broadway Cruise Ship Dock

Cruise Ship Terminal

Cruise Ship Terminal

State Ferry Dock

The Mascot Saloon is now part of the Klondike Gold Rush National Historical Park.

ports of Dyea and Skagway. The first stampeders arrived in Skagway in August 1897. A tent city quickly sprang up. During the two years of the Klondike Gold Rush, over 100,000 stampeders would be infected with "Klondicitis." Newcomers were called *cheechako* ("tenderfoot" or "greenhorn"). Experienced prospectors were dubbed "sourdoughs," because they often used sourdough starter as the yeast in bread and flapjacks.

Skagway quickly became a lawless boomtown where bunco artist Jefferson Randolph "Soapy" Smith and his gang of hoodlums and "sure thing" men fleeced unwary cheechakos as they arrived, and robbed successful sourdoughs returning from the Klondike. The sound of occasional gunfire mingled with the neighing of freight teams and the whine of Billy Moore's sawmill. More than 700 new frame structures rose above the original tents in the first four months of the rush. Every week at least two steamships arrived freighted with optimistic men and women planning to hike over the White Pass from Skagway or the Chilkoot Pass from Dyea. Both routes scaled the 6,000-foot coastal range that separates the Canadian interior from the American coast. Moore put the word out that White Pass was lower than the Chilkoot, and that since it was clear of boulders (unlike the Chilkoot), pack animals could take food and supplies all the way from tidewater to Lake Bennett. And then it was just 450 miles to Dawson and the gold fields.

Klondike prospectors and their goat-drawn sled of supplies, ca. 1898.

A December 31, 1897, article in *The Skaguay News* by Annie Hall Strong encouraged women to join the stampede. Strong claimed she expected to find "mobs of evil-doers" but instead found "everything orderly and quiet . . . no evidence of violence or crime—nothing but kindness." There were 3,000 people in town as Strong wrote, and the insta-burg boasted a church, a school, electric lights, and a telephone system.

The newspaper's articles acted like press releases from a chamber of commerce on speed: "Here we can glorify and jollify with the full assurance that in no spot in the entire Union does the bright sun of prosperity beam more effulgently and with greater radiance than here in Skaguay, the metropolis of the northwest, the marvel of the last decade of the nineteenth century." Professional photographers including Eric A. Hegg, H. C. Barley, and Asahel Curtis captured dramatic moments along the trails and in lonely diggings, making the Klondike Rush the most-photographed event of the century. Magazines and newspapers from around the world dispatched reporters for first-hand stories.

The reality was far from bright and wholesome. In the summer of 1898 some 15,000 people were living in tents, shacks, and crude rooming houses. Skagway had 61 saloons, an equal number of gambling dives, three breweries, and dance halls from which drifted tunes like "There'll Be a Hot Time In The Old Town Tonight." Specialty acts like knife throwers, acrobats, trained dogs, female singers and dancers, and magicians were imported to amuse miners—and separate them from their dust and nuggets. Superintendent Samuel Steele of the Royal North West Mounted Police described it as "the roughest place in the world, little better than a hell on earth."

Steele was particularly infuriated by Soapy Smith. The con man was a skilled sleight-of-hand artist with a variant on the usual walnut shells and hidden pea game; he used bars of soap, hence the nickname. Gold-mad Skagway offered in spades the ingredients Soapy needed to work his swindles—desperate men in a strange land and a swift population turnover. Soapy operated out of a saloon staffed by a bartender in a white jacket. This "parlor" fronted for marked-card games, muggings, robberies, and murders all the way from the docks to the White Pass.

After Soapy Smith was shot dead in a duel in July 1898, life in Skagway became safer and even rather civilized. Newspaper ads turned from miners' supplies and portable Yukon stoves to bathtubs and "fine toilet seats." In 1900 the newly constructed White Pass & Yukon Railway to Lake Bennett promoted itself as the "Scenic Route of the World," and the Pacific Coast Steamship Company assigned

ON THE CHILKOOT TRAIL

After a wonderful night's sleep, a hearty breakfast of cornmeal mush, bacon, and cold-storage eggs, condensed milk, prunes, and a whole orange—the last in the camp—and settling our hotel bill (meals and bunk $1 apiece), with high hearts that glorious July morning we started to climb that 3,000 feet of steep, narrow, icy mountain trail. The Indians said there was a curse on all who attempted it in summer, as the hot sun melted the winter snow, and it came crashing down. These avalanches had already taken toll of nearly 100 lives.

For the first hour we walked over the trail of the recent slide. In the melting snow I saw a bit of blue ribbon. Bending down, I tugged at it and pulled out a baby's bootee. Did it belong to some venturesome soul who had come to seek a fortune for wife and baby? Would those who were waiting for him wait in vain?

I did not dare look round at the magnificent mountain scenery nor drink in the beauty of the tumbling torrents, for every minute the melting snow was making it more slippery under foot.

As the day advanced the trail became steeper, the air warmer, and footholds without support impossible. I shed my sealskin jacket. I cursed my hot, high, buckram collar, my tight heavily boned corsets, my long corduroy skirt, my full bloomers which I had to hitch up with every step. We clung to stunted pines, spruce roots, jutting rocks. In some places the path was so narrow that, to move at all, we had to use our feet tandem fashion. Above, only the granite walls. Below, death leering at us . . . . In my agony I beg the men to leave me—to let me lie in my tracks, and stay for the night.

—Flo Whyard (ed.), Martha Black: *Her Story from the Dawson Gold Fields to the Halls of Parliament*, 2003

three ships to the summer Alaskan tourism trade. With its population at 15,000, Skagway was at this time the largest city in Alaska.

When the rush to the Klondike dwindled and stampeders headed instead to destinations such as Nome and Fairbanks, the population of Skagway quickly

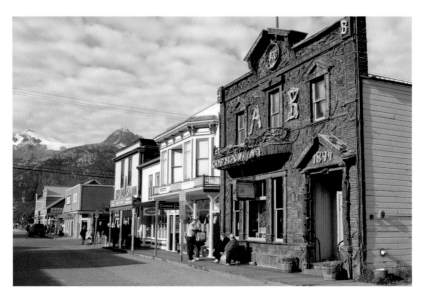

The Arctic Brotherhood Hall, where members gathered for "fun, fight, or footrace."

declined. By 1910 there were only a few hundred residents. Gold production in the Yukon fell off through the 1930s, and gold mines in Alaska were shut down during World War II. But military storage at Skagway helped to keep the town going through the war.

SKAGWAY NOW *map page 119*

Although Dyea has become a ghost town, Skagway thrives, a beehive of tourist activity—at least for half the year. In fact, many Skagway sites remain much the same as they were in the hectic days of 1897–98, right down to the false fronts that pretend one-story buildings rise to two stories, the wooden sidewalks, and the gleaming dome of the Golden North Hotel (1898). Billy Moore's cabin is still here, as is Jeff Smith's Parlor, although both have been moved to new locations. The original, one-story Brackett's Trading Post (1897) was moved to Broadway and restored in the 1980s by the National Park Service. The neat network of streets remains as it was laid out by surveyor Frank Reid—the man who shot Soapy Smith in a confrontation on one of the town's wharfs.

Following page: Skagway tourists then (the turn of the 20th century) and now.

Victims of circumstance in Dyea's Slide Cemetery.

An example of Skagway's commitment to preserving history is the ★Klondike Gold Rush National Historic Park. This park was established in 1976 after decades of local lobbying. It's an unusual setup, split between Washington and Alaska. The northern segment includes Skagway's historic structures, the deserted Dyea townsite, the White Pass Trail to the boundary with Canada, and the first 17 miles of the Chilkoot Trail. Another special link to the past is the White Pass & Yukon Railway. After a hiatus in the 1980s it relaunched its passenger service from Skagway to Lake Bennett and is now a top visitor attraction.

Skagway is renowned for its gardens. Long hours of "midnight sun" and the dew that accumulates during the evening stimulate speedy growth, especially of fragrant sweet peas, enormous dahlias, and tart, rosy rhubarb. Fair weather is likely here, as precipitation in Skagway averages a mere 26 inches a year—but keep a scarf handy for the wind.

This tight-knit community has 864 year-round residents, but played host to 900,000 visitors in 2007. It may sound like Six Flags Over Skagway, and there's no denying summer crowds, but the town's careful restoration is impressive. To bypass the high-season throngs, try for the "shoulder season" in early May or late September. But keep in mind that the weather may not be as cooperative

KID STUFF

- Count the pieces of driftwood on the front of the **Arctic Brotherhood Hall.** During the winter of 2004/05 the city repaired, restored, and replaced 8,000 of the 20,000 chunks of driftwood on this structure—one of the most-photographed in town.

- Combine trains and flowers at **Jewell Gardens** (Klondike Highway; 907/983–2111). Just over the bridge crossing the Skagway River, the showy garden includes flowers, organic vegetables, and a model railroad. The G-scale railroad winds through a model town that resembles Skagway in Soapy's day, complete with a tent city. While you watch the trains puff-puff into tunnels, you can sit down with a proper cup of English tea, a wedge of smoked salmon quiche, or a nasturtium sandwich with herbed cream cheese.

and that some of the souvenir shops close as the owners head to Tucson or Hilo for the winter.

WALKING TOUR

The big draw is the **Klondike Gold Rush National Historic Park** (907/983–2921; www.nps.gov/klgo), where you can walk in the footsteps of Captain Moore, Soapy Smith, and Jack London.

The best place to walk is the downtown Skagway historic district section of this park. Take a self-guided tour of the 15 restored buildings by scanning the map available at the White Pass & Yukon Railroad Depot at Second Avenue and Broadway. In summer, rangers give 45-minute tours daily, but it's pleasant to simply follow your nose. The historic building at Broadway and Seventh, now the Skagway Inn Bed & Breakfast, was established as a brothel in 1897. You'll find the Ben Moore House at Fifth Avenue and Spring Street. Be sure to pause for the 30-minute film, *Days of Adventure, Dreams of Gold,* for an overview of life here during the gold rush.

The visitor information center is in the **Arctic Brotherhood Hall** (245 Broadway, near Second Ave.; 907/983–2854). The structure is unmistakable—

studded with pieces of driftwood. Built in 1899, this hall was headquarters for a secret fraternal organization whose members gathered for "fun, fight, or footrace." To learn more about town history, sit and research at the **Skagway Museum & Archive** (Seventh and Spring Sts.; 907/983–2420). (This was formerly known as the Trail of '98 Museum, and is sometimes referred to as the "City Museum.") Exhibits and photographs cover all the highlights, like Moore's first crude wharf and sawmill, the tumult of the gold rush, the life and death of Soapy Smith, the railroad, and World War II. Native objects include a Tlingit canoe from Klukwan, carved halibut hooks, a bentwood box, and a Chilkat blanket.

Plan on about three hours for this walk; a visit to the Skagway Museum will require another hour.

BRIEF EXCURSIONS

Attend the **Days of '98** show (Eagles Hall, Broadway and Sixth; 907/983–2545), a raucous musical melodrama based on Skagway's early history. Dramatis personae include Soapy, Molly Fewclothes, and Squirrel Tooth Alice. In other words, this is a bawdy eyeful. Performances begin at 8 PM daily in summer, preceded by an hour of gambling demos.

The ★**Gold Rush Cemetery** is two miles from downtown. It's a walk on level ground, straight up State Street from the waterfront. Most of the graves in this quiet, wooded setting date from 1898 to 1904, and included are the markers for Soapy Smith and Frank Reid. Some of Soapy's critics didn't want him buried here, but the local reverend—to whose church he had made a sizable donation—insisted he be in consecrated ground. **Flightseeing tours** via helicopter are available, with spectacular views of glaciers and crevasses or a visit to Lake Bennett. Routes include tours of the Ferebee, Chilkat, or Meade glaciers—or dogsledding on the Denver Glacier. Allow about two hours for this outing. Among the major local operators are Skagway Air (907/983–2218; www.skagwayair.com) and TEMSCO Helicopters Inc. (907/983–2900 or 877/789–9501; www.temscoair.com).

Dyea was originally a Tlingit settlement guarding the trailhead for the Chilkoot, a prized trade route. The overgrown **Dyea Town Site** is nine miles northwest of Skagway. Rangers offer 1½-hour walking tours of this ghost town from mid-May through September, but don't provide transportation to the site. (If you don't have a car, try a cab, though these can be hard to find. Or you could rent a bike and ride, if you don't mind bumpy gravel.) Register for the tour at the Historic Park. There's not much to see at Dyea other than wharf pilings, mysterious clear-

Bawdy performers at the Red Onion Saloon.

ings among the evergreens, and the Slide Cemetery. A Palm Sunday avalanche in 1898 smothered at least 60 argonauts, and many who died in it are buried here. Legend has it that Soapy sent his henchmen to pick the corpses' pockets as they awaited burial.

LONGER OUTINGS

If you don't mind breathtaking heights, board the narrow-gauge ★White Pass & Yukon Route Railway (800/343–7373; www.whitepassrailroad.com) for a three-hour excursion to rocky, 2,900-foot White Pass. You ride in cars from the mid-20th century; an interpreter in each car discusses the scenic highlights, like Bridal Veil Falls. In order to feel like a fly on a cliff face, sit on the left side leaving Skagway and on the right when returning. Fog occasionally rolls in, but most of the time unobstructed views are spectacular. The tour is available from May through September; because of its popularity, make reservations well in advance.

Sign up for a **day hike with Packer Expeditions** (907/983–2544). Packer leads guided hikes in the area, including day and multiday hikes. Its most popular excursion is a 5½-hour jaunt involving a helicopter flight over the Juneau Ice Field; a four-mile hike to Laughton Glacier; and a WP & YR ride back to

HUBBARD GLACIER

The Hubbard Glacier is an icy tongue with its root near 15,300-foot Mt. Hubbard in Yukon Territory; it flows 76 miles to lick the sea at Yakutat and Disenchantment bays. Many people access the glacier by floatplane from Skagway, Haines, or Yakutat. With its 400-foot snout, Hubbard Glacier is also a prime pausing point for cruise ships. Hubbard calves great numbers of icebergs, making it difficult to get close. (There are no roads to the glacier.)

Yakutat, a town on the Gulf of Alaska, 225 miles northwest of Juneau, has some draws of its own. The scenery's magnificent, and there's world-class sport fishing for cutthroat trout, Dolly Varden, and salmon. The "Tat" (the river's nickname) is famed for white water. And you can certainly get away from it all, as there are no roads to Yakutat and the Alaska Marine Highway ferry stops there only when it has vehicles to unload.

The 24-million-acre wilderness around Hubbard can only be described with superlatives. For example, the massive St. Elias and Fairweather ranges are the largest nonpolar glaciated mountain system in the world. The region supports both grizzlies and rare, silver-blue "glacier" bears.

This glacier is famous for "surging"— moving forward quickly. Most glaciers slide an inch or two a day. However, in 1986, the Hubbard Glacier made headlines around the world by advancing to the mouth of Russell Fiord, damming it, and creating a huge lake that lasted five months. By September it was advancing 30 meters a day. This was an event without precedent in recent geologic history.

Seals, sea lions, and porpoises were trapped behind the dam, and efforts were mounted to relocate them. "Russell Lake" eventually reached a level almost 90 feet higher than the level of Disenchantment Bay. When the dam broke on October 8 it produced an enormous rush of fresh water— something like a tidal wave in reverse.

The glacier surged again in summer 2002, creating another dam in the space of a month—by coincidence, just about the time glaciologists convened in Yakutat for an international symposium on fast glacier flow. Nervous Yakutat residents continue to lobby the government to build a channel to make sure the glacier cannot form "Russell Lake" again. They fear this would change river courses, endanger fisheries, and inundate the Yakutat Airport, the chief transportation link with the rest of Alaska. For more on the current state of the Hubbard, see the U.S. Geological Survey site (http://ak.water.usgs.gov).

Skagway. Packer provides all gear, water, and snacks. Wear sunglasses to guard against glacier glare.

Take a hike from the Dyea trailhead over the ★Chilkoot Pass Trail (www. nps.gov/klgo/chilkoot.htm). The entire Chilkoot trail is 32 miles and peaks at 3,246 feet. It crosses from Alaska into Canada, with fascinating variations in habitat along the route. It's also a mile-wide "museum," as you'll see boot soles, horse bones, enamelware coffeepots, collapsible canvas boats—all things that overburdened stampeders discarded on their way to Dawson City. You can photograph these, but cannot disturb them. It's a challenging hike; you'll need to negotiate snaking roots, slippery rocks, and mud. The "Golden Stairs" section stacks boulders the size of railroad cars and smaller rocks that shift unnervingly underfoot. The arduous trek takes most fit folk three to five days. Camping is restricted to locations where cook shacks are provided. While you won't have to haul a year's worth of supplies over the pass, as 1897–98 stampeders did, you will need to shoulder a tent, grub, and fuel. Bring rain gear, plus cords and a storage sack to hang your food out of reach on bear poles. Before hiking in, check with the Historic Park for the latest information on trail conditions and to get instructions for Canadian customs, which maintains an office at the top of the pass. It's difficult to get anyone in Skagway on the phone during peak hours, so make your inquiries well in advance.

FAVORITE PLACES TO SHOP AND EAT

At the **Corrington Museum of Alaskan History** (Broadway and Fifth Ave.; 907/983–2580), you can tour a scrimshawed version of Alaska's past. Painstakingly etched walrus tusks and carved ivory models commemorate historic events. Up front, the gift shop sells videos of Alaska's scenery plus the usual souvenirs.

For a little hot stuff, try glassblowing a garden ornament at **Garden City Glassworks** (Mile 1 Klondike Highway, at Jewell Gardens; 907/983–2111). Inspired by a class with internationally known glass artist Dale Chihuly of Seattle, this is the only Alaska glassblowing studio that is open to the public. Enjoy lunch, beer or wine, and watch the experts, or attempt the art yourself. The $150 per-person fee includes one ornament and lunch.

Stowaway Café. The Stowaway haggles directly with local fishermen in order to serve the freshest seafood possible. One sample dish is wasabi salmon, crusted with panko (Japanese breading) and broiled. The café is also known for its freshly baked bread and homemade soup. *205 Congress Way; 907/983–3463. Closed Oct.–Apr.* **$–$$**

H A I N E S

Haines is set on Portage Cove, a gentle curve in the shoreline of Lynn Canal. Like Skagway, Haines is a compact spot, with a downtown half a dozen blocks wide and half a dozen blocks deep, although there are "suburbs" slowly rising in the direction of Chilkoot Lake and Battery Point Trail. The only high-rises are the natural backdrop—the jagged, 6,500-foot Cathedral Peaks. These make a stunning "stage set" for the dress parade of white clapboard officers' residences at Fort William H. Seward.

Some tourists hurry through on their way to what they consider "bigger fish" like Kluane National Park. But Haines is worth an overnight stay. For one thing, Haines is one of the drier spots on the Inside Passage, averaging 2 inches of precipitation per month during the summer. Around the summer solstice you can expect about 20 hours of daylight during which to explore.

Haines is a rarity—an Inside Passage town connected to other road systems. The Haines Highway follows the general route of a packhorse trail to the Klondike used by prospectors in the late 1880s. This 44-mile highway connects Haines with Haines Junction in Canada's Yukon Territory. When the threat of invasion from Japan appeared after Pearl Harbor, the road was improved for military access. If you drive the route now—a trip of about an hour—you can observe coastal rain forest gradually give way to alpine tundra.

HAINES THEN

The first humans to settle in the Chilkat Valley were Tlingits. They seem to have established a site at Klukwan, 22 miles up the Chilkat River. A second large settlement was established near Chilkoot Lake, five miles north of the modern ferry dock. Before 1881 there was nothing permanent at the site of modern Haines—just a summer fish camp with temporary shelters and fish-drying shacks slightly to the northwest. At this fish camp, called Dei Shu, or "end of the trail," Chilkat and Chilkoot Indians traded first with Russian and then with American ships.

In addition to the fish runs, bald eagles may have been part of the area's attraction for the Chilkoot and Chilkat tribes. Eagles are an important Tlingit cultural symbol; eagle down was often scattered during potlatches. The Tlingits established important trade routes into the interior. These were called "grease trails" because

A rare road along the Inside Passage: the Haines Highway.

The Klehini River and Takhinsha Mountains northwest of Haines.

the most valuable item carried over them was eulachon or hooligan oil, rendered from small fish that run each May. (Hooligan are so oily that they're nicknamed "candle fish," because you can insert a wick into a dried fish and use it like a candle.) The grease, stored in hollow kelp or bentwood boxes, was exchanged for copper, obsidian, and furs.

In 1879 naturalist John Muir and his friend Presbyterian missionary S. Hall Young scouted the area with the help of Tlingit guides. Two years later, Young assigned two Presbyterians to found a mission, which was named for a Presbyterian fundraiser, Francina Haines. Muir was stunned by the sheer bulk of spawning salmon he saw here: "Their numbers are beyond conception. Oftentimes there seem to be more fish than water . . . . Surely in no part of the world may one's daily bread be more easily obtained." Canneries naturally followed in 1882, with up to nine operating at the peak of the industry.

Anticipating gold rushes in the interior, American entrepreneur Jack Dalton "mined the miners" by turning a grease trail into the Yukon into a 305-mile toll road. He began construction in 1891; eventually the trail linked Pyramid Harbor (west of Haines) with Fort Selkirk on the Yukon River. Dalton established trading posts along his trail, and by 1899 the U.S. government had granted him permission to charge fees. However, by 1900 competing routes established by miners reluctant to line Dalton's pockets put Dalton essentially out of business.

Fort William H. Seward—named after the U. S. secretary of state who championed the Alaska Purchase—stands on a knoll half a mile south of downtown Haines. The fort was proposed in 1902 because of an ongoing border dispute

FAQs

What's the connection between Haines and Darth Vader?

Actor James Earl Jones, the voice of Darth Vader in *Star Wars*, commissioned a totem from Alaska Indian Arts of Haines. The 22-foot pole, completed in 2001, has a four winds design in homage to Jones's Choctaw heritage.

Where are the bald eagles?

The local quipster's reply is "look up." Truth is, during the summer eagles fade away to a variety of feeding spots. But in autumn they concentrate around Haines in large numbers. The Alaska Chilkat Bald Eagle Preserve is considered one of Alaska's top ten visitor destinations.

What are the names of the two glaciers you see from the ferry deck about 40 minutes out of Haines?

The first one spotted along the shores of the fjord called Lynn Canal is the Davidson Glacier. The Rainbow Glacier comes next. Both icy tongues flow out of one of the ice fields of Glacier Bay National Park.

A frosty catch of coho, or silver, salmon in the Chilkat River, near Haines.

A gold rush–era trading post, ca.1895–1897.

between the United States and Canada. When it was completed in 1904, it became the first permanent army post in Alaska and was considered "foreign-duty." If you're arriving by water, you'll spot its distinctive white Victorian-style officers' quarters as you approach town.

Haines was incorporated in 1910. In the early 1920s Haines, like many small, struggling frontier towns, competed for settlers, printing leaflets trumpeting its attractions. In 1924 Haines tooted its own horn with a large sign across its main street: "Haines, Alaska, is the natural gateway to Porcupine, Rainy Hollow, White Run and Tanana valley, have Vast Resources of gold, silver, copper, lead, iron, and coal. Large areas of farming, grazing, and timber lands. Best climate of any city or town on the coast of Alaska." That year the population was about 300. Tlingits were employed at a cannery seven miles out of town, and there was a saw-mill half a mile north. Like most communities along the Inside Passage, Haines was accessible only by sea and air until a flurry of war-related construction linked it to the rest of the world by road in 1943.

After World War II the decommissioned fort was sold to a group of veterans. Mimi and Ted Gregg and Carl Heinmiller were among those offered homesteads, and, captivated by Haines, they made a gutsy decision. They recognized that

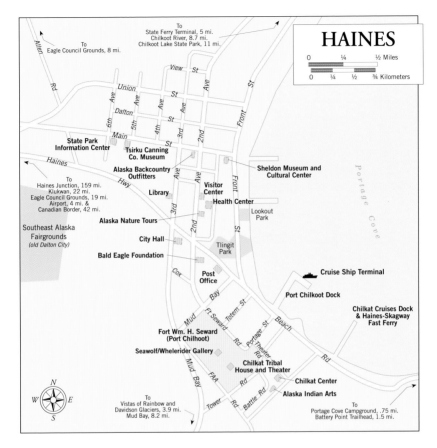

To State Ferry Terminal, 5 mi.
Chilkoot River, 8.7 mi.
Chilkoot Lake State Park, 11 mi.

To Eagle Council Grounds, 8 mi.

HAINES

0   ¼   ½ Miles

0   ¼   ½   ¾ Kilometers

Allen Rd

View St

Union Ave

Dalton St

6th Ave

5th Ave

4th Ave

3rd Ave

2nd Ave

Front St

Main St

State Park Information Center

Tsirku Canning Co. Museum

Alaska Backcountry Outfitters

To Haines Junction, 159 mi.
Klukwan, 22 mi.
Eagle Council Grounds, 19 mi.
Airport, 4 mi. &
Canadian Border, 42 mi.

Haines Hwy

Library

Visitor Center

Health Center

Sheldon Museum and Cultural Center

Lookout Park

Alaska Nature Tours

Southeast Alaska **Fairgrounds**
(old Dalton City)

City Hall

Bald Eagle Foundation

Tlingit Park

Post Office

Cox Bay

Mud Bay Rd

Ft Seward Rd

Totem St

Portage St

Theater Rd

Beach Rd

Cruise Ship Terminal

Port Chilkoot Dock

Chilkat Cruises Dock & Haines-Skagway Fast Ferry

Fort Wm. H. Seward (Port Chilhoot)

Seawolf/Whelerider Gallery

Chilkat Tribal House and Theater

Chilkat Center

Alaska Indian Arts

FAA Rd

Tower Rd

Battle Rd

To Vistas of Rainbow and Davidson Glaciers, 3.9 mi.
Mud Bay, 8.2 mi.

To Portage Cove Campground, .75 mi.
Battery Point Trailhead, 1.5 mi.

N W E S

Portage Cove

Tlingit tradition was fading and resolved to establish training programs to preserve Tlingit arts, including woodcarving, sculpture, lapidary work, and Native dance, adding block printing and textile design. The hospital became home to Alaska Indian Arts, and programs continue to this day.

HAINES NOW *map page 137*

Fewer cruise ships dock here than in Juneau or Skagway, so the mood is serene. As Lee Heinmiller (Carl's son) puts it, "It's an actual real community—not Knott's Berry Farm of the North." Several stately homes along Officers' Row have been recycled as bed-and-breakfasts, where you can sit on the porch, admire the gingerbread moldings, and smell the lilacs or sweet william. Haines author Heather

THE SCALPEL AND THE AX

There is a huge scientific debate raging in the Tongass over what kinds of windstorms may have begotten the forest we see today. In some places, huge gales occasionally sweep the forested mountain slopes, leaving twenty-acre piles of felled trees. A study of one island on the Tongass suggested that these intense storms may have affected a sizable percentage of the area—providing a perfect excuse for those who favor massive clear-cuts to say their logging is simply an emulation of nature. But the forest tells a much more complex story. It is not a large patchwork like a nice orderly tapestry we might want to weave, but a mosaic, every piece a different shape, each overlapping some others, and all with a different story of disturbance. If only we could more easily adopt the view of one of these patriarchs, it would be so much easier to see what is important, what is the scalpel and what is the ax, where and how often each force plays a role, and to what ultimate effect.

—Paul Alaback, "The Tongass Rain Forest—An Elusive Sense of Place and Time," in *The Book of the Tongass*, 1999

Lende calls her home "a small town where everybody waves and you don't have to lock your doors." The population hovers at about 1,800.

Haines is to bald eagles what Pack Creek is to brown bears. The stately birds flock to the Chilkat Valley because the warm open water of its rivers and its spawning salmon make for a comfortable food source well into cold weather. As the salmon finish spawning in fall, they begin to die off—the perfect eagle meal. Several hundred eagles live here year-round, but an additional 3,000 feed here October through January, resulting in the world's largest gathering of eagles. The Alaska Bald Eagle Festival celebrates this event for a week every November. The best place to watch the eagles is at the Alaska Chilkat Bald Eagle Preserve (*see* Brief Excursions, *below*). There's also an eagle museum downtown that offers opportunities to bone up on the birds.

The jagged Cathedral Peaks set off the tidy buildings of historic Fort Seward.

Haines is set on gentle Portage Cove.

Fishing is an angler's delight. Drive to sites like Chilkat State Park (7 miles south of Haines on Mud Bay Road), Chilkoot Lake State Recreation Site (12 miles north of Haines, off Lutak Road), and Mosquito Lake State Recreation Site (about 30 miles north of Haines along the Haines Highway). All three sites have fire rings, toilets, potable water, picnic tables, and a boat launch. Dolly Varden bite year-round. In the fjord, fishermen hope for salmon, halibut, rockfish, and lingcod.

Haines is a base from which to travel to Glacier Bay, Skagway, or the Yukon. Alaska Marine Highway ferries stop here on their trips north from Bellingham, Washington. Skagway is just 35 minutes away by water taxi (catamaran) from mid-May to mid-September. And there is a daily 2½-hour ferry service from Skagway (Haines-Skagway Fast Ferry; 888/766–2103).

LET THE MASK BUYER BEWARE

From the first days of trade between explorers and Northwest Coast peoples, art played a role. Indians at Nootka Sound, in British Columbia, left masks on board visiting ships—apparently as gifts. One captain described this occurrence: "Natives would sometimes bring strange carved heads and place them at a conspicuous part of the ship and desire us to let them remain there, and for this they would receive no return." Both Captain James Cook (1778) and Captain George Vancouver (1792) carried cedar masks, daggers, rattles, basketry, and intricately carved fishhooks back to England. The masks were realistic, dramatic, and colorfully painted. Museums were delighted to have them.

Masks are still avidly collected for their aesthetic appeal. However, buyers should beware of copies created in production workshops in Bali and other countries. Balinese carvers use reference books to research traditional Tlingit, Eskimo, Kwakiutl, and Haida designs. In other words, "bargains" are sometimes not good deals but imported copies by non-Natives. An artist's signature is no guarantee, because workshops make a practice of purchasing the rights to Native names or coining Native-sounding names.

Take precautions: Ask for a certificate of authenticity. Buy directly from carvers working on-site or from Native artists with their own galleries. Those who know Pacific Northwest or Inuit art well may recognize a copy if it looks out of proportion or wears nontraditional colors. Black, red, brown, yellow, blue-green, and white paint are long-established colors, but pink, blue, or orange paint aren't in the traditional palette.

If a shop owner refers to a "local artist," he may mean a Canadian rather than an Alaskan. If clerks insist on playing 20 questions about the identity of an artist, thank them—and move on.

Another tip: Inspect each mask carefully. If carved from green wood, it may have hairline cracks in several places.

Chilkat dancer, ca. 1955.

If you begin at the Port Chilkoot Dock, walk along the beach or turn right on Beach Road. Admire the **Welcome Totems Park**, where poles depict bears, eagles, and salmon. Turn left on Main Street, go two blocks, and then make another left on Second Avenue to check in at the **Haines Convention & Visitors Bureau** (122 Second Ave. South; 907/766–2234). If you plan to see Fort Seward, pick up the free pamphlet *A History and Walking Tour of Fort William H. Seward*. From here, turn right on Second Avenue and return to Main Street. Turn right again and keep an eye peeled for the **Hammer Museum** (108 Main St.; 907/766–2374), where hundreds of antique and modern hammers speak to one man's esoteric fascination. A block away is the **Sheldon Museum & Cultural Center** (11 Main St.; 907/766–2366). The Sheldon's displays focus on Tlingit art and culture typical of the area, the Haines Mission, and pioneer history. The museum's collection is based on objects collected by pioneers Steve and Elisabeth Sheldon, who married here in 1913. As you leave the Sheldon, turn left onto Main and head to the ★**Tsirku Canning Company Museum** (Fifth and Main Sts.; 907/766–FISH). Observe a restored canning line in action; all the equipment dates from the 1920s.

This would be a good time to break for lunch. (There are several casual lunch spots downtown.) Afterward, if you're still raring to go, head left down Main Street toward Portage Cove, then turn right on Front Street. Take a detour into the small boat harbor to snap some photos, if you wish, or continue along Front (which parallels the shoreline) until you reach Portage Street. Turn right on Portage Street, then curve left on Second Street, and **Alaska Indian Arts** will be on your left (24 Fort Seward Dr.; 907/766–2160; www.alaskaindianarts.com). AIA has been an important force in the revival and perpetuation of Northwest Coast art and performance since 1947. The organization's home base has a cultural history display, plus printmaking. Watch totem carvers, Chilkat blanket weavers, and silversmiths at work. Prints, weavings, and silver jewelry can be purchased, and totems can be commissioned.

Known as "The Post," **Fort Seward** was built as a showplace of Army strength on the frontier. Italian stone masons were imported to cut foundations from local granite, and local spruce became clapboard. More than 90 buildings rose, including an ice house, stables, and telegraph office as well as officer housing. Vegetable gardens supplied produce. The chief surgeon's house has become a bed and break-

KID STUFF

- Fans of big bangs should take in the unique **Hammer Museum** (108 Main St., uphill from the harbor; 907/766–2374). About 1,500 hammers are on display—from mighty implements for forging swords to tiny tack hammers for upholsterers. You can lift a few, including a two-handled beauty. Kids 12 and under get in free.

- Strap on that imaginary Colt 45 and explore **Dalton City,** the set for the movie *White Fang*, at the Southeast Alaska State Fairgrounds, off the Haines Highway about ⅓ mile from downtown. It's like walking a frontier street of the 1890s, though the buildings are reproductions.

- For close encounters with indigenous wildlife such as lynx, wolves, pine marten, moose, collared lemmings, and woodland caribou, visit **Kroschel Park** (Mile 1.5, Mosquito Lake Rd., 30 miles north of Haines; 907/767–5464). This 60-acre sanctuary is the baby of Steve Kroschel, and his stock is mostly orphaned, hand-raised young 'uns. Kroschel once took a wolverine on the *Tonight Show*. Species that need extra room, such as wolves, are kept in large compounds. There are usually some animals that can be touched, such as the Arctic fox.

- As dazzling as Broadway's *The Lion King* are the puppets, staging, costumes, and lighting integrated in the **Chilkat Dancers Storytelling Theater** (Totem Village Tribal House, Fort Seward Parade Field; 907/766–2540). The legends presented are straight from elaborate, traditional winter ceremonials. Kids can enjoy weekday afternoon performances for $6.

fast. Stroll the grounds or call naturalist/photographer Joe Ordonez for a custom tour (907/766–3576; joeorga@hotmail.com).

This walk would take roughly five hours, including a lunch break.

BRIEF EXCURSIONS

The ★**Alaska Chilkat Bald Eagle Preserve** (Haines Hwy.; 907/766–2292; www.dnr.state.ak.us/parks/units/eagleprv.htm), created in 1982, spreads its protective wings over 48,000 acres bordering the Chilkat, Klehini, and Tsirku riv-

(top left) Bald eagles flock to their feeding grounds. (bottom left) And photographers follow them. (above) More than 3,000 eagles gather in the Chilkat Valley from October through February.

Salmon fishing on the Chilkat River.

ers. Logging and mining are illegal here, but the harvesting of naturally replaced resources such as berries and fish is permitted. The best observation areas are accessed from pullouts along the Haines Highway, between 18 and 26 miles from town. At mile 18, there's a mile-long trail that includes accessible boardwalk lined with interpretive signs.

There is nothing like being on the riverbank in December as mists curl upward and thousands of screaming eagles fight over salmon carcasses. (Eagles have several calls, including a high fluting cry that definitely gets your attention.) If you're here in spring, especially April, you'll have a good chance of seeing the spectacular courtship behavior, when the birds lock talons in flight and cartwheel earthward.

To learn more about eagles before you go, visit the **American Bald Eagle Foundation** (113 Haines Highway; 907/776–3094; www.baldeaglefest.org). This education center displays a diorama of the Chilkat preserve, taxidermied specimens, and a video.

Hike to the summit of 1,760-foot **Mount Riley** for superb views of Lynn Canal, Taiya Inlet, and the Chilkat River. Read the *Haines is for Hikers* brochure (available at the visitor center) before you head out. The short, steep route (2

EAGLES AND RAVENS

Along the Inside Passage, eagles and ravens are not simply regal, high-soaring creatures. They're also symbols of the two main divisions of Tlingit society—as meaningful as donkey and elephant to Democrats and Republicans. The Tlingit word for "eagle" is *ch'aak*—which sounds something like a cry the eagle makes. The Tlingit word for "raven" is *yeil*. A hundred myths lie behind the raven's jet stare.

Mature eagles with their white heads and tail feathers are the largest, most visible of the 300 bird species that live here. Their wingspans stretch between six and eight feet; the females are slightly larger than the males. About half of all bald eagles in the world live in Alaska. About one quarter of those, or 10,000 breeding pairs, construct their large platform nests along the Inside Passage. Amended year after year, a nest can weigh 2,000 pounds. Although carefully hidden, most nests are within 200 yards of water, so that the parents can be close to fishing grounds for the 70 to 90 busy days spent feeding their chicks.

How can you tell a raven from a crow? Although both are sleek and black, the raven is larger and has a more massive bill. While crows flock in groups of up to 50 birds, ravens tend to be solitary or fly in pairs. The Tlingit considered ravens to be very intelligent, clever, and even tricky.

Bold and curious, a raven has a confident stride and is not easily spooked. Ravens will eat almost anything, from sea urchins to roadkill porcupines. They have 17 distinct calls—expressing messages such as "humans approaching" and "lots of food over here."

Although they compete for some of the same foods, ravens and eagles may mingle to "kettle." This is flying in a languid spiral, taking advantage of mountain updrafts.

Both raptors appear in Tlingit art, especially as masks or on totem poles. A raven is carved with a straight beak, while an eagle's beak is curved or hooked. A certain type of Chilkat blanket with black tassels is known as the "raven's tail." Look for these birds in the designs beaded on ceremonial vests and headbands too.

miles) begins 3 miles southeast of Haines on Mud Bay Road. The long, less difficult route (4 miles) begins on FAA Road behind Fort Seward.

August visitors can head to the **Southeast Alaska State Fair** (Dalton City; www.seakfair.org). Events include a women's logging show, a Most Lovable Dog contest, and a songwriters' competition. Kids gravitate to the carousel, game booths, and a fire-eating clown.

LONGER OUTINGS

A quiet spot where three rivers meet, ★**Klukwan**, "Mother Village," is one of the only inland settlements in Southeast Alaska, and it's a treasure trove of Tlingit art—probably because it was too far from the coast to be shelled by the military or exploited by museum representatives. Its center is the Gaanaxteidi clan dwelling, Killer Whale Fin House. Discussions over how to allow visitors to see clan artifacts without interrupting the daily life of the 160 villagers continued for decades. To raise funds for a museum, elders like John Katzeek allow limited access. Keet Gooshi Tours can take you there (five-person minimum; 907/767–5770). *Keet Gooshi* means killer whale, and John was born into the tribe. The tour includes a ride through the Alaska Chilkat Bald Eagle Preserve, a visit to the tribal house, storytelling, and a demonstration of the preparation of "Indian butter" (eulachon grease) in the Traditional Knowledge Camp.

The **four house posts** in the Killer Whale Fin House are the well-preserved work of the genius Kadjisdu.axtc, or "The One Who is Listened To." Carved in the early 1800s, the posts are Raven & Bullhead, Chief's Daughter, the sea creature Konakadet, and Duk Toothl (Black Skin). The central figure of the latter is a sea lion and man merged. The posts are considered the Northwest's *Mona Lisa*. When the tribal house in which they stand decayed, it was replaced with a milled lumber replica in 1899. A hospitality house and museum are in the works, with the entire complex scheduled for completion by 2011. The trip to Klukwan takes four to five hours.

Hard bodies are drawn to Haines for its kayaking and glacier-hiking opportunities. Get a taste of the action with half-day, full-day, or overnight **sea kayaking excursions** with Alaska Mountain Guides & International Wilderness Leadership School (907/766–3366; www.alaskamountainguides.com). AMG offers mountain climbing instruction out of Skagway, and in Haines they offer 12- and 24-day instructional jaunts leading to wilderness leadership certification.

Take a guided float trip on a multi-day **river expedition** on the Tatshenshini, Alsek, or Kongakut rivers with Chilkat Guides (907/766–2491;

www.raftalaska.com). If you're short on time, sign up for the four-hour float trip on the Chilkat River.

Venture into Canada to visit the Yukon's **Kluane National Park and Reserve** (www.parkscanada.gc.ca/kluane), three hours north of Haines via the Haines Highway. Its St. Elias mountains will have you goggling. Woodland caribou sometimes stand in the road, Dall sheep clamber about, and there are 150 bird species, including the golden eagle. Adventurous visitors are attracted by the white water for which the Alsek River is famous. You'll need your passport to cross the border; your vehicle may be inspected for firearms or carved ivory. Canadian Customs is at Pleasant Camp, Mile 40.8 (907/767–5540). If traveling between September 15 and June 1, be sure to check on weather conditions (Alaska State Troopers in Haines, 907/766–2552; or Royal Canadian Mounted Police in Haines Junction, 867/632–5555). Be prepared for snow and ice.

FAVORITE PLACE TO SHOP

Tresham Gregg, born in Haines, creates art invested with what he calls "spiritism." Items range from cooking spatulas to totems, from plaques to bronzes, silk screen prints, talismanic silver jewelry, lamps, jackets, and masks. Gregg's gallery, **Seawolf/Whale Rider** (center of Fort Seward, in a trapper's cabin surrounded by totems; 907/766–2540), also stocks African Krobo trade beads.

FAVORITE PLACES TO EAT

Mountain Market. Track lights set off the brick-red, purple, and butterscotch interior of this café and natural food store. Walls display paintings by locals (for sale, naturally). The menu has panini, tortilla wraps, daily soup, and scones. Try the cranberry muffins, and for a pick-me-up, the espresso bar. (Beans are roasted in-house.) The owner guarantees "no animals on the walls, but they're sometimes in the parking lot." *151 Third Avenue South; 907/766–3340.* **$–$$**

Hotel Halsingland. Founded by Swedish immigrants in a decommissioned building on Fort Seward, this is Haines's only full-service restaurant. Top draws include the potato bar and fresh seafood dishes, such as blackened salmon and crab dip served with house-baked Parmesan-fennel crackerbread. Before your meal, set the mood by sipping a Fort Seward Howitzer in the Victorian lounge. *Fort parade grounds; 907/766–2000.* **$–$$**

A cruise ship negotiates the watery maze of Glacier Bay.

GLACIER BAY
NATIONAL PARK AND PRESERVE

Red rivulets on a drifting ice floe at Johns Hopkins Glacier reveal that a harbor seal has just given birth. Suddenly the mother seal barks hoarsely. Tall, menacing black fins circle the floating nursery. Orcas, "wolves of the sea," angle for a tender pup lunch.

At the terminus of the Grand Pacific Glacier, birds wait for ice to calve so that they can feed on the shrimp and krill churned up by the turbulence. Mountain goats clamber up steep rock faces. Sea otters float on their backs in the surrounding water, cracking open clams with rocks.

Such activities are as much a part of the world of Glacier Bay as the polished rock marked by gouges or grooves called "glacial footprints." Naturalist John Muir wrote of this ecosystem, ". . . out of all the cold darkness and glacial crushing and grinding comes this warm abounding beauty and life to teach us what we in our faithless ignorance and fear call destruction is creation finer and finer."

GLACIER BAY THEN

Glacier Bay was once home to the Huna Tlingit. They arrived in the bay 3,500 years ago, but the Little Ice Age drove them out. Legend has it that as it drove away the Tlingit, the ice surged "faster than a dog could run," called down by a grumpy girl in puberty seclusion. The Tlingit name for the bay is *Sit'ee ti geiyi,* or "place where the ice used to be." There's truth behind the legend. Several cycles of glaciation have occurred in this region. The Tlingit then settled at Hoonah. Their cultural memories of the bay's rich resources—delicious seabird eggs, for example—remain strong.

This magnificent, 3.28 million-acre maze of inlets, islands, and glaciers was solid ice a mere 200 years ago. In July 1794 the HMS *Discovery* under the command of Captain George Vancouver was forced to drop anchor in Cross Sound because of the floating bergs in the area. Vancouver sent two longboats to survey, and his men sighted a five-mile-long bay. The 60-mile bay we know today was then just an indentation plugged by a cork of ice 300 feet high and five miles wide.

Researching theories about glaciers that he had coined in Yosemite, John Muir first saw the bay in 1879, describing it as an "icy wildness unspeakably pure and sublime." In a Tlingit dugout canoe Muir explored a bay 48 miles long. Since about 1750 the bay has grown into a glittering nest of ice, with 12 tidewater gla-

GLACIER BAY
NATIONAL PARK
AND PRESERVE

| 0 | | 5 | | 10 Miles |
| 0 | 5 | | 10 | 15 Kilometers |

1794 Historical extent of glaciation

Muir Glacier

Riggs Glacier

Carroll Glacier

Renda Glacier

Renda Inlet

Tarr Inlet

1976

1972

1960
1948

1966

1929

1966

1892

1929

1907

Casement Glacier

Queen Inlet

Wachusett

1966

1949

Adams Inlet

1892

1892

1880

RUSSELL
ISLAND

Muir Inlet

Lamplugh Glacier

Reid Glacier

1907

1892

1907
1892

1879

1907

1919

Geikie Inlet

1892

1860

1907

1892

1860

Glacier

Bay

Inlet

1857

1845

DRAKE
ISLAND

Beartrack River

Brady Icefield

1966

1892

West
Lake

WILLOUGHBY
ISLAND

Beartrack Cove

BEARDSLEE ISLANDS

Brady Glacier

Abb

Dundas
River

Berg
Bay

Visitor Center
Glacier Bay Lodge

Park
Headquarters

1794

Bartlett Cove

Airport

1750-80

Gustavus

Pleasant
Island
Wilderness

1961

PLEASANT
ISLAND

Dundas Bay

North Passage

Icy

Strait

Dixon Harbor

Graves Bay

Taylor Bay

LEMESURIER
ISLAND

N
W   E
S

Cape Spencer

Inian
Islands
Wilderness

INIAN
ISLANDS

South Passage

CHICHAGOF
ISLAND

The lucky few who gain access to Glacier Bay will find an extraordinarily well-preserved environment.

FAQs

What is "bergy seltzer"?
Bergy seltzer is the fizzing noise made when air that has been under pressure escapes from bubbles in glacier ice. It's also called "ice sizzle." Often cruise ships net a chunk of ice to give that "snap, crackle, pop" to preprandial cocktails.

What is the meaning of "Hoonah"?
It means "village by the cliff."

Why is some glacier ice blue?
The blue of glaciers derives from the pressures exerted on ice crystals during formation. As the crystals morph, they absorb longer light wavelengths and reflect back only short wavelengths, the blue end of the visible light spectrum. Glaciers appear bluer on overcast days—and they're easier to photograph when it's cloudy too. Blue ice becomes white as it is exposed to oxygen.

THE GLACIER AS ARCHIVIST

A glacier is an archivist and historian. It saves everything, no matter how small or big, including pollen, dust, heavy metals, bugs, bones, and minerals. It registers every fluctuation of weather. A glacier is time incarnate, a moving image of time: when we lose a glacier— and we are losing most of them—we lose history, an eye into the past; we lose stories of how living beings evolved, how weather vacillated, why plants and animals died. The retreat and disappearance of glaciers—there are only 160,000 left—means we're burning libraries and damaging the planet, possibly beyond repair. Bit by bit, glacier by glacier, we're living the Fall.

—Gretel Ehrlich, *The Future of Ice: A Journey into Cold*, 2004

ciers, 30 alpine glaciers, and at least a dozen unnamed glaciers flowing out of the St. Elias Mountains into the arms of the bay. The land was designated a National Monument in 1920, a National Park and Preserve in 1980, and a World Heritage Site in 1992.

GLACIER BAY NOW *map page 154*

The community of **Gustavus** (pop. 450), 48 miles west of Juneau, sits on a glacial moraine deposited as ice receded. "Downtown Gustavus" is the proverbial whistle stop—minus the train. Beartrack Mercantile is the sole grocery store. The community lacked electricity until 1990, and composting toilets and outhouses were the general rule until this century. But it's not utterly spartan here; there are several luxury lodges and B&Bs. The airport was built in the 1940s to fuel military aircraft, because the weather here is often clearer than it is in Juneau. The airport structures perch at the eastern edge of the moraine, while Park Service Headquarters, a campground, Glacier Bay Lodge, and the boat dock line Bartlett Cove at the western edge of the moraine, nine miles from anything else.

More than 438,000 people visited Glacier Bay in 2007—although large cruise ships do not stop. The National Park Service preserves the extraordinary marine environment by limiting entrance, and only two large ves-

It's virtually impossible not to get a good glacier shot.

sels are permitted a day. ("Large vessels" are motor vessels of 100 U.S. gross tons or more carrying paying passengers.) Whoever lines up the best visitor programs wins the bidding process for these entry slots. Cruise ships in the preserve are generally from the Princess or Holland America lines; they offer interpretive programs, carry rangers on board, and organize children's programs. Smaller tour boats can also jockey for admission; Alaska Sightseeing/Cruise West generally nets those slots. Permits run from midnight to midnight, so no vessels stay overnight. To become more intimately acquainted with the bay, arrange for flightseeing, fly-out sport fishing in Icy Strait, or guided kayak trips. Visitors usually yearn to hear the impressive "boom" of calving, when ice chunks break off the glacier faces. Calving is unpredictable, but any cruise guarantees a firsthand lesson in the cycle of plant succession.

When glaciers melt away, they expose bare rock. Traveling up Glacier Bay, you'll virtually head back in time, witnessing the succession from the mature forest of Bartlett Cove to the naked earth at Margerie Glacier. After ice retreats and exposes bare rock, plant recovery begins with a black crust of algae. Next come horsetails and fireweed. As soil accumulates, willows and alders take hold. At the culmination of the process, hemlock and spruce trees soar 200 feet into the blue.

Steller sea lions basking on South Marble Island.

Weather stirs the pot. Storms boil in off the Pacific, and when it rains on the bay it's snowing on the Fairweather Range, including the dramatic peaks of Fairweather (15,300 feet) and Mt. Crillon (12,726 feet). This snow builds up, compacts, and in 150 to 200 years gains enough weight to flow down from the mountaintops as a glacier. The glaciers here are retreating, though, and the warmer temperatures and shrinking ice seem to be spurring tourism. Some estimates guess that this national park's glaciers could vanish by 2030.

Air taxis, Alaska Airlines jets, and a three-times-weekly ferry access Gustavus during the summer. Air Excursions will fly you over from Juneau for $70 one-way. For details, contact the Gustavus Visitor Association (907/697–2454; www.gustavusak.com) or Glacier Bay National Park Headquarters (907/697–2230; www.nps.gov/glba).

BRIEF EXCURSIONS

Shake those sea legs along the two **hiking trails** near Glacier Bay Lodge. One is a mile-long nature loop. The other is the Bartlett Cove Trail, three miles round-trip. The latter offers a gander at the only mature spruce forest in Gustavus, the result of 200 years of plant succession since ice backed away from this terminal moraine. Fallen trees show the force of winter gales. Many of these now serve as horizontal "nurse trees," with saplings growing in the rotten wood, all in a row.

Take a **whale watch and wildlife cruise** with Cross Sound Express (888/698–2726) to Point Adolphus and Icy Strait. The 3½-hour tour has two departures a day. Underwater microphones let you listen in on the songs of humpback whales. Orcas, harbor porpoises, Steller sea lions, and sea otters are frequently sighted. In business since 1972, Discover Alaska (800/586–1911) also offers brief trips to see the whales of Point Adolphus.

Flightseeing trips over the Brady Ice Field and Fairweather Range are available with Air Excursions (907/697–2375) or L.A.B. Flying Service (907/789–9160). During an hour's excursion, the plane lands in front of a glacier or on a beach studded with aquamarine bergs.

LONGER OUTINGS

Because foot travel in the park is limited to beaches, moraines, and rocky avalanche chutes, **kayaking** is one of the best ways to explore. "Living with the tides" is the M.O. here. Squalls come and go; tarps are put up and taken down. Both Discover Alaska (800/586–1911) and Glacier Bay Sea Kayaks (907/697–2257;

Margerie Glacier offers front-row seats for the first stage of the plant succession cycle.

www.glacierbayseakayaks.com) are licensed to operate in Glacier Bay. Excursions in Icy Strait or Glacier Bay range from a half day to 14 days.

Kayakers can guide themselves to the Beardslee Islands near Bartlett Cove for a day or overnight trip. Moose regularly swim to and from the Beardslees—and orcas sometimes nab a snack of moose. Campers are required to attend an orientation at the visitor information center before departure.

Most visitors make time for the all-day ★tidewater glacier trip on the park concession boat *Spirit of Adventure,* a stable catamaran that seats 200 in comfortable, heated decks. A Forest Service naturalist discusses all the sights, from seabird rookeries to sea otters. The boat stops near the Canadian border, swiveling back and forth between the 250-foot-high terminuses of the Margerie and Grand Pacific glaciers. The Grand Pacific grinds through softer rock, presenting a dirty face to the world. The Margerie is cleaner and whiter.

S I T K A

Sitka lies on the west side of Baranof Island, about 95 miles southwest of Juneau. Its name means "people on the outside of the island." Legend says that the Kiks.adi (the dot indicates a swallowing sound in the throat for which English has no equivalent) Tlingit paddled here in prehistoric times seeking a village site, towing a wooden frog emblem behind one of their canoes. Sitka had all they needed: fish (especially a spring herring run), game, timber, berries, seaweed, and other resources.

Sitka's two harbors look out on the pleasant prospect of more than a hundred evergreen-topped islands. To the west rises the cone of Mt. Edgecumbe, an extinct volcano often compared to Mt. Fuji. Although Sitka is not technically on the Inside Passage, Kruzon Island protects Sitka Sound from the largest Pacific swells. The waters here are an important summer feeding ground for whales, sea otters, and sea lions. The climate is mild, if damp—with many more sunny days than Juneau. The town is just the right size to explore on foot. Streets radiate out like spokes of a wheel from the golden dome of the Russian Orthodox church. Instead of lemonade, kids sell Russian wedding cookies from folding tables. Stroll along shady Lincoln Street, enjoying the breeze off Crescent Harbor, licking powdered sugar from your fingers—perfect!

SITKA THEN

Sitka's original inhabitants, the Kiks.adi Tlingit, established trading relationships with other nearby Native communities, using seagoing canoes to reach the Haida to the south and Copper River Ahtna to the north. Spanish navigator Juan Perez may have been the first European to attempt to land near Sitka. In 1774 Perez bartered for fresh water with the Kiks.adi.

In the late 18th century the Russians moved in, under the command of the resilient, charismatic Alexander Baranof (1746–1819), the chief manager of the Russian-American Company. Russia hoped to control the trade in sea-otter pelts, and to that end, in 1799, Baranof led a flotilla of 300 kayaks and two ships south from Prince William Sound. Waves swallowed 30 kayaks en route, and there were skirmishes with the Kolosh, but Baranof pressed on, traveling at night. He was met at Sitka Sound by a large crowd of Kiks.adi and their chief, Skayeutlelt. Baranof bargained for land upon which to build a post, christened Archangel Michael (now Old Sitka).

A trio of peaks overlooks Sitka, ca. the early 1900s.

Baranof described the Kiks.adi Tlingits as "numerous, strong and audacious." He and his men survived the winter, and by the following spring they had built a fortified garrison housing a company of 450, mostly Aleut otter hunters and their wives.

In June 1802 Skayeutlelt, egged on by his nephew Katlian, turned on the Russians in what is sometimes called the Sitka Massacre.

The Tlingit planned the attack carefully. Conspirators included Haida chiefs from the Queen Charlotte Islands, as well as Tlingit chiefs from five other tribes. On a Sunday afternoon, when some of the garrison men were fishing or berry picking, the warriors suddenly emerged from the forest armed with guns, spears, and daggers. One description of the battle claims there were over a thousand attackers. Of the 450 men, women, and children at the garrison, only 42 survived.

SITKA

0   ¼   ½ Miles

0   ¼   ½   ¾ Kilometers

Peterson Ave

Verstovia St

Halibut Point Rd

Lake St

Thomsen Harbor

Lakeview St

Swan Lake

Monastery St

DeGroff St

Sitka National Cemetery 1867

Indian River Rd

Sawmill Creek Rd

Sitka Channel

Marine St

Kaatlan St

Russian Bishop's House

Biorka St

Oja St

Etolin St

Jeff Davis St

Baranof St

Monastery St

Lake St

Japonski Island

To Airport Terminal

Airport Rd

Russian Blockhouse Replica

Sheet'ka Kwaan Naa Kahidi Tribal House

Sitka Pioneers' Home

Seward

Lincoln St

St Peter's by-the-sea Episcopal Church

To Whale Park 2 Mi

Sealing Cove

Totem Square

Post Office

Centennial Hall/ Sitka Historical Museum

College

Kelly St

Metlakatla

Sitka National Historical Park

Castle Hill

O'Connell Bridge

Harbor Dr

St Michael's Cathedral

Sheldon Jackson Museum

Crescent Harbor

Totem Poles

Sitka Rocky Gutierrez Airport

Turning Island

Mitchell Rock

Cruise Ship Anchorage

Sitka Sound

N
W   E
S

Sitka has a busy waterfront—but one thing you won't see is a cruise-ship dock.

FAQs

What materials go into a Chilkat blanket?

This ceremonial robe is woven of mountain goat wool and yellow cedar bark. Fringes of wool decorate the lower edge. Men create the designs; women twine them into the robe.

What is frybread?

Frybread is a Native American dish sometimes called "the Indian tortilla." It developed when flour, bread dough, and frying were introduced to Eskimo, Tlingit, Apache, and Navajo. It resembles pita or pocket bread, and is best served warm from the skillet. Pick up its scent at fairs and during holiday weekends. Frybread is often served drizzled with honey or topped with pinto beans, lettuce, tomato, and cheese for a hearty "Indian taco."

Why was Sitka called the "Paris of the North Pacific"?

From a rustic outpost, Sitka transformed itself into a cosmopolitan port where ships were built and launched. Particularly after 1840, when the talented linguist and inventor Bishop Ivan Veniaminov was in permanent residence, scholarly and scientific pursuits began to replace some of the rowdier fur-trader elements. The town had a library, a museum, a meteorological observatory, and a hospital. Balls were held, and wealthy ladies imported the finest fashions from New York, London, St. Petersburg, and Paris for such occasions.

Sitka is a mother lode of Native arts and crafts.

Guests at a Sitka potlatch, ca. 1904.

Baranof mobilized his forces. He returned in 1804 with a fleet of 300 kayaks, 800 Aleut hunters, 120 Russians, and 4 small ships. The *Neva*, a warship under the command of Urey Lisiansky, met him at Sitka Sound. Lisiansky had his cannon installed on a raft so they could get even closer to the Tlingit fortifications. At first the Tlingit seemed to hold their own. In a magnificent helmet, Katlian stalked the beach wielding an iron blacksmith's hammer and a double-ended dagger. But gradually force of arms won out, and the surviving Tlingit escaped into the forest.

Baranof erected a new fort on the site of the vanquished Tlingit stronghold, later called "Castle Hill." He called it New Archangel. Conditions were bleak, and the men constantly manned the palisades, ready to repulse another attack. The deadlock continued until Baranof was about to retire in 1818, when Katlian came to bid him farewell. "Now we are old men together and about to die, let us be brothers," Katlian said.

MISSIONARIES AND BUSINESSMEN

Unlike the maritime fur traders, the missionaries and industrialists who arrived in the second half of the nineteenth century came to live on a long-term basis. They deliberately sought to influence the customs and beliefs of the Natives. The missionaries brought a new religion, schools and a new language. The businessmen brought a new economic system. Caucasian settlement of the Northwest Coast meant that new material goods were available to the Indians. In some ways, the material standard of living increased greatly. However, to earn money to buy the goods, Indians had to take jobs and participate in the new economy. Whether or not they intended to work together, the missionaries and the businessmen influenced the Northwest Coast people in similar ways.

. . . missionaries sought to suppress the potlatch celebrations. Missionaries fought the potlatches for a number of reasons. They feared the drinking and the unsanitary conditions that began to characterize the celebrations after Caucasians introduced the Natives to alcohol. Employed Indians abandoned their jobs to participate in the potlatches. School attendance plummeted. Some missionaries felt that feasting Natives squandered food that they needed to hoard during the winter months. Finally, the potlatch played a strong role in passing myths and customs to the younger generation, and reinforced traditional economic and social structures.

—Victoria Wyatt, *Shapes of Their Thoughts: Reflections of Culture Contact in Northwest Coast Indian Art,* 1984

Baranof knew he could not rid the region of competition from American traders. So he did the next best thing: he divvied up with them. In 1809 he made a share agreement with the Americans or "Boston men." Five years later he made a similar agreement with the Pacific Fur Company, owned by John Jacob Astor. As the town prospered, a barracks, a customs house, a Russian Orthodox seminary, two schools, and a governor's "castle" were built, and a foundry and sawmill began operating.

During its Russian heyday in the early 19th century, Sitka was the busiest port on the eastern shore of the Pacific, and the only shipyard north of Hawaii. It shipped ice from Swan Lake to San Francisco during the California Gold Rush. The administrative headquarters for Russian America followed Baranof from Kodiak to Sitka. While all this high living was taking place on one side of the stockade, on the other side the Tlingit lived in sorry conditions, facing a battery of eight Russian cannon.

Little changed for the Kiks.adi, according to authors Richard and Nora Dauenhauer. "The Russians were not strong enough to undertake a full-scale occupation of Tlingit country," they write in *Haa Kusteeyi, Our Culture,* "and the areas beyond the fort at Sitka remained in Tlingit control. For the most part, the traditional Tlingit social system remained intact, and the Tlingit were not disturbed in their traditional use of the land and its resources." But for many years, diseases such as smallpox tore through the Tlingit population.

Tlingit crafts registered the social shift. Instead of large burden baskets and hats of cedar bark and spruce root, weavers began turning out souvenir items such as recycled wine and medicine bottles covered with basketry. Rather than working in copper, Tlingit artisans hammered silver dollars into brooches, bracelets, and spoons, some decorated with the American eagle from the coin itself rather than traditional split, two-dimensional, symmetrical "form line" designs.

Bishop Ivan Veniaminov, who visited Sitka in 1834 and settled there in 1840, made major strides in converting Natives to Christianity. He made efforts to develop a writing system for various Native languages, introducing Natives to the Russian Orthodox teachings but also, in the end, helping to preserve these oral languages. For schoolchildren in Sitka, he prepared bilingual textbooks himself, with parallel texts in Tlingit and Russian. He also urged vaccinations against Western diseases. (Vaccination and conversion often went hand in hand.)

As the sea-otter-pelt trade waned, Russia approached the United States with an offer to sell its Alaskan land. The agreement was signed in Washington, D.C., on March 30, 1867. The Americans took formal possession on October 18, 1867, during a ceremony on Sitka's Castle Hill. A Navy man, C. D. Bloodgood, reported on the immediate influx of opportunists: "Before our first sunset gun was

(top, at right) The Cathedral of the Archangel Michael speaks to the 19th-century Russian community. (bottom, at right) The view down Lincoln Street in the early 1900s. Native women selling souvenirs have set up shop under the trees.

fired, their preempting stakes dotted the ground, and ere long they had framed a city charter, devised laws and remunerative offices, and by an election, at which less than one hundred votes were mustered, gave publicity to, and inaugurated their schemes. Their squatter claims were confirmed and recorded." The Tlingit were not permitted into Sitka to witness the transfer ceremonies. They could only stand on the beach beyond the palisade in their separate enclave, the "Ranche."

Administration of "Seward's Icebox" or "Walrussia" was turned over to the War Department. An artillery regiment established garrisons at Sitka, Wrangell, and Tongass. For decades, the only law in Alaska consisted of orders issued to the Commanding General. He was directed to "impress upon the Indians and especially upon their chiefs, that our government will regard them as subject to its laws and entitled to its protection; that while they are protected by our government they will be required to respect the rights of all citizens of the republic." In other words, Native Americans were not citizens. To be considered for citizenship, they were required to lead a "civilized life"—a term interpreted variously by the authorities.

Jefferson Davis, Commanding General in 1867, visited Tlingit and Haida villages, warning the residents against molesting white men. Before these meetings, some Natives had been unaware of the sale of Alaska and objected to the transaction on the grounds that the Russians had no right to sell Tlingit land.

In 1878 John Green Brady arrived in Sitka as a missionary, staying to turn businessman and politician. The fifth governor of the District of Alaska, Brady collected 15 Haida totem poles and a 54-foot war canoe for the Alaska exhibit at the Louisiana Purchase Exposition held in St. Louis in 1904 and the Lewis and Clark Exposition in Portland a year later. The poles became the basis for Sitka National Monument.

Sitka hummed along quietly until Pearl Harbor. The Navy then fortified Japonski Island, building a base with 30,000 military personnel. This armed camp just offshore had a huge impact on the culture and economy of the town. Today the U.S. Coast Guard maintains facilities on Japonski, and a bridge connects the island with the mainland. The major postwar economic player was the Alaska Lumber and Pulp Company. Its main timber facility closed in 1993—another shock from which the town is still recovering.

KID STUFF

- Bring crayons. A **junior ranger activity book** about Sitka National Historical Park is available to children 4 and up at the park's visitor center (106 Metlakatla St.; 907/747–6281).

- Visit a wild bird hospital, the **Alaska Raptor Center** (1101 Sawmill Creek Rd.; 907/747–8662), where injured bald eagles, golden eagles, hawks, owls, and falcons are rehabilitated. The eye-dazzler here is the 20,000-square-foot flight-training center, designed to look like a rain forest. Watch exercising birds through one-way glass. The center is an easy 10-minute walk from Sitka National Historical Park.

SITKA NOW *map page 164*

Picturesque Sitka brims with history—Tlingit, Russian, Alaskan. The town's architectural centerpiece is the Russian Orthodox cathedral at the head of Lincoln Street. Its historic centerpiece is Sitka National Historical Park, established in 1910. The park's 113 acres include a visitor center and the Southeast Alaska Indian Cultural Center, as well as the site of the Tlingit fort and 1804 battlefield, the Russian Bishop's House, a memorable loop trail lined with totems, and a memorial to Russian midshipmen who died in the battle.

The Tlingit "Ranche" has still not been completely absorbed into the "Russian side" of downtown, an example of the enduring tensions between Natives and non-Natives throughout Alaska. The Alaska Native Claims Settlement Act of 1971 helped to bridge the economic gap to some degree, but grudges and prejudices simmer not far beneath the surface on both sides. The reproduction log blockhouse overlooking downtown seems an ironic reminder of this tension.

One thing all Sitka's strong-minded population (just under 9,000) values is the town's history. Putting the beauty of their waterfront ahead of commercial development, residents have opposed a downtown cruise-ship dock. As a result, at this writing all cruise-ship passengers are tendered to shore.

A TLINGIT SAMPLER

As visitors to Hawaii hear words like *mahalo*, visitors to Sitka may hear *gunalcheesh*. Thirty percent of Sitka's population is Tlingit, and cities like Juneau and Sitka offer Tlingit immersion classes in elementary schools.

Wasa-i-yatee (pronounced *wasa-ee-ya-tee*): "How are you?"

Yak'ei (*yuk-ay*): "Good."

Ax-xooni (*ach-hoonee*): "My friend."

Igu-ayax-xwan (*ee-gooayug-won*): "Be brave."

Gunalcheesh (*gun-nush-cheesh*): "Thank you."

Hit (*hit*): Clan house, as in Yehlh hit, "Raven's House."

Dis or disi (*disee*): month or moon, as in Tahwak disi, "goose moon."

Keet (*keet*): killer whale.

Sha (*sha*): mountains.

Xoots or Hootz (*kootz*): brown bear; or as in the proper name Anna Hootz, "Brown bear country," a Ka-gwan-tan chief's name at Sitka.

Kootznoowoo (*kootz-nu-wu*): "Fortress of the brown bears." The name for Admiralty Island.

Hoonah (*who-nah*): "The place where the north wind doesn't blow."

WALKING TOUR

Starting where cruise-ship passengers come ashore, on Harbor Drive near the O'Connell Bridge, head into town on Harbor. You can make a detour to the left to see Castle Hill, or see it on the way back.

Make a left on Observatory Street to reach the domed **Cathedral of the Archangel Michael** (Lincoln and Seward Sts.; 907/747–8120), sitting regally in its own little circle of streets. Under the direction of Veniaminov, its foundation was laid in 1848, in the shape of a cross. The vaulted interior is laid out in the Orthodox manner, with the sanctuary separated from the public area by a gilded screen called an iconostasis. This partition is adorned with 12 icons with silver adornments. The central door leading to the sanctuary is called the Royal

Sitka has the largest harbor system in the state of Alaska.

Gates; through this ceremonial portal the Eucharist is brought out to the faithful. Today's cathedral is a reconstruction; the cathedral suffered a fire in 1966. However, the present structure was built from the plans of the original, and residents managed to save many antique religious items now on display.

From the cathedral, walk along Lincoln Street to the **Sitka Convention & Visitors Bureau** (upstairs, 303 Lincoln St.; 907/747–5940), a trustworthy source of information. Then continue along Lincoln about two blocks to the ★**Russian Bishop's House** (Lincoln and Baranof Sts.; 907/747–6281). This is a rarity—one of only four original colonial Russian structures remaining in North America. The two-story log structure, built in 1843, contains the refurbished quarters of Bishop Veniaminov with a private chapel. (Veniaminov was canonized by the Orthodox Church as St. Innocent.) Exhibits illustrate the Russian fur trade in Alaska and the roles of the Russian-American Company and Russian Orthodox Church. It opened to the public in May 2008.

Get a handle on how Sitka looked under Russian rule by viewing the scale model at the **Sitka Historical Museum** in the Harrigan Centennial Building (330 Harbor Dr.; 907/747–6455). The museum focuses on the shared history of Russian, American, and Tlingit residents.

There's no missing Mt. Edgecumbe, an extinct volcano.

The ★Sheldon Jackson Museum stands at a seeming driveway that is at right angles to Lincoln Street, on the Sheldon Jackson College campus. Built in 1895, the museum (104 College Dr.; 907/747–8981) displays the state's oldest continuously exhibited collection of Native art and artifacts, including shamans' gear and totems. The eponymous missionary-educator Reverend Dr. Jackson gathered his collection between 1888 and 1898. His museum was the state's first fireproof and the first concrete structure. One treasure is the helmet that Katlian, the Tlingit war leader, wore during the battle of 1804. It is carved from a knot of wood covered with bearskin and topped with a raven whose eyes are inlaid with copper. Pull out and investigate the drawers with glass lids that hold special treasures such as children's toys from several cultures.

The walk thus far requires about four hours. If you still have stamina, press on around the curve of Lincoln Street to Sitka National Historical Park, about an eighth of a mile away (*see* Brief Excursions).

BRIEF EXCURSIONS

Explore ★ Sitka National Historical Park (end of Lincoln St.; 907/747–0110), a 113-acre preserve that includes the site of the Tlingit fort and the 1804 battle with the Russians. Outside the visitor center's front door stand large contemporary totems that record Tlingit history. Inside the center is the **Southeast Alaska Indian Cultural Center**, which houses both a museum and workshops. During the summer you can watch Native craftspeople beading, making jewelry, and carving wood. The 10-minute slide show *Battle of Sitka* helps explain precisely what happened here in 1804. Exit the back door and take the self-guided tour along a one-mile wooded path, where spruce trees arch overhead and ravens evermore yawp in the branches. Totem poles are spaced along this path—a favorite with locals. (The forest trail is wheelchair accessible.) The rocky shore of Sitka Sound paralleling the totem path is a pleasant place to sit and listen to the waves for a spell, or to take a picnic. Marvel at Sitka's wonderfully clean air.

Koo.eex'—that is, welcome to a ceremony at which both Eagles and Ravens will be in attendance. The tall panels flanking the entrance to the **Sheet'ka Kwaan Naa Kahidi Tribal House** (200 Katlian St.; 907/747–7137) represent the Eagle and Raven moieties. Drummers set the beat and a songleader gives the commands, as dancers in outfits of deerskin, felt, feathers, and intricate beadwork circle the floor. Some dancers wear frontlets (masks at forehead level) or face-covering masks, while others twirl and stomp in Chilkat blankets or button blankets.

THE TONGASS

The Tongass National Forest is 17 million acres of green, the largest national forest in the United States. Set aside in 1907, the preserve—approximately the size of West Virginia—encompasses about 90 percent of Southeast Alaska.

Under the management of the U.S. Forest Service, it has been designated "multiple use." Rather than being reserved solely for logging or mining, it is used for logging and mining, plus recreation. Greenpeace regularly anchors one of its larger ships in ports along the Inside Passage and gives visitors tours and information about the issues involved in forest management. It's a contentious issue. Small Alaskan towns need jobs, and lobby for logging. Residents of larger towns criticize the way clearcut forests look and how long it takes them to recover.

The cool, damp, temperate rain forest of the Tongass supports species such as red and yellow cedar, western hemlock, and Sitka spruce. Resistant to insects, Sitka spruce can live to be 700 years old and 200 feet tall. Native peoples harvested Sitka spruce logs to build their plank houses, totems, and canoes. They also gathered spruce roots and bark for weaving and used devil's club (a thorny plant related to ginseng) for medicine.

The early Russian emigrants harvested trees at Sitka to build ships. When American steamships carried tourists to Alaska, they took on firewood felled in what is today the Tongass. Those logged-over areas have grown back. During World War I spruce was requisitioned by the military to build aircraft. In World War II spruce was used for gliders. Little wholesale logging took place until after World War II.

But the Tongass is not just trees. It encompasses glaciers, mountains, lakes, islands, straits, and channels. And there is an exceptional abundance of wildlife here. Bald eagles make the Tongass their home. Black and brown bears live here, as do Sitka black-tailed deer, mountain goats, beavers, lynx, wolves, wolverines, red foxes, river otters, great blue herons, little brown bats, porcupines, martens, the northern goshawk, the marbled murrelet, red and flying squirrels, and weasels. Both saltwater and freshwater fish flourish here too, including the five Pacific species of salmon.

From Tongass gateway towns such as Ketchikan or Sitka you can take self-guided hikes, bike tours, or guided Jeep excursions on back roads. A sojourn at a remote cabin is a way to get up-close-and-dazzled. The Tongass has 145 cabins, 80 of them accessible from Ketchikan. For information, go to www.fs.fed.us/r10/tongass.

Their dress—not "costumes"—may include *at.oow*, colorful regalia showing clan crests. Performances are given against a backdrop of two carved house screens, giving a strong impression of what a potlatch celebration would have looked like in the late 1800s. The 30-minute dances are scheduled mostly in summer.

LONGER OUTINGS

Saltwater fishing is high on many must-do lists, especially since statistically the chances of hooking into a king are excellent. Saltwater angling is at its best June through August. The most common catches are king, silver, and pink salmon, halibut, and ling cod. A list of charter operators is available from the Convention & Visitors Bureau (907/747–5940).

You can arrange for a three-hour **wildlife-spotting harbor tour** with Annahootz Alaskan Adventures, in search of sea lions, humpbacks, sea otters, and brown bears (907/747–2608).

For a more leisurely time, try **a weeklong wilderness tour** on a converted commercial vessel with Coastal Wilderness Adventures (800/287–7063). The ship is equipped with kayaks (beginners welcome) for exploring the shoreline up close or venturing into the Chichagof Wilderness.

Board Alaska's only semi-submersible tour vessel to get **an underwater look at Sitka Sound** with Sea Life Discovery Tours (877/966–2301). Jellyfish, waving forests of kelp, anemones, and sea stars are common sights. Trips are available for either 1½ or 2 hours.

FAVORITE PLACES TO SHOP

The tiny shop of the **Cathedral of the Archangel Michael** (*see above*) offers icons in many sizes. **Sheldon Jackson Museum's** (*see above*) attached shop is an excellent place to seek out jewelry and crafts—objects an aesthetic cut or two above "souvenirs."

The Russian-American Company (407 Lincoln St., second floor of Bayview Trading Company; 907/747–6228) is piled high with lacquer boxes illustrating Slavic fairy tales, Russian dolls (both freestanding and nesting), Fabergé jewelry, Christmas decorations of layered birch bark, *pysanki* (Easter eggs), and antique samovars. (Russian-American operates a Juneau shop, "Grandfather Frost," which offers much the same wares.)

The Sitka Rose Gallery (419 Lincoln St.; 888/236–1536) stands next door to the Russian Bishop's House. It gives you a chance to enter a century-old residence and also to browse among sculpture by Jacques and Mary Regat of

Anchorage, plus paintings, beadwork, and jewelry. Willis Oseakken grew up in this house; he specializes in Tlingit bentwood boxes, spoons, and paddles. Cathleen Pook works with antique beads, while Susan Stanford makes her own glass for jewelry. The wood block etchings of Eric Bealer of Pelican are some of the shop's most popular items.

FAVORITE PLACES TO EAT

Ludvig's Bistro Inc. This bistro serves dinner only, from 4 to 10 PM Monday through Saturday, in an intimate setting serving 30. The atmosphere is Old Europe, with European art displayed. The menu reflects owner Collette Nelson's apprenticeships in Pacific Northwest Italian restaurants as well as her travels in Spain and around the Mediterranean. You can nibble on tapas before digging into fresh king salmon or paella. Nelson buys her seafood "right down the street." Her paella blends rockfish, calamari, prawns, smoked salmon, and imported Spanish chorizo and chicken. *256 Katlian St.; 907/966–3663.* **$–$$**

    Westmark Sitka. Both the Kadataan Lounge and the Raven Dining Room in this modern, upscale hotel focus on seafood, all purchased locally if possible. Try the blackened or cedar-planked salmon. Kadataan offers a casual sports bar atmosphere, while Raven brings out the tablecloths and wineglasses for formal dinner service. Start with the bacon-wrapped scallop appetizer. Then choose among the no-hormone steaks, the King crab leg special, or true cod and chips. True cod was introduced because of the rising prices of halibut. *330 Seward St.; 907/747–6241 or 800/544–0970.* **$$–$$$**

PRACTICAL INFORMATION

ANIMAL- AND BIRD-WATCHING

Be prepared: Bone up on habitats, behavior, and migratory patterns *before* the target creature waddles or flaps into view. To field questions about particular species, get in touch with the Forest Service Information Center in Juneau (907/586–8751; www.fs.fed.us/r10/tongass). Whether you seek falcons or mamots, bring binoculars. (Some cruises and tours, as in Glacier Bay National Park, supply pairs for the length of the trip.) Adept at spotting game, resident naturalists and skippers will point out animals and birds, then maneuver as close as allowable.

Dial up WildLifeWatcher.com for info on the best time to visit specific sites to increase the odds of sighting favorites. Birdzilla.com offers bird touring information.

BEARS

Black and brown (grizzly) bears are most visible from May through September near food sources such as berry patches and avalanche chutes lush with edible greens. Bruins leave forest cover to take advantage of spawning salmon. Odds are good in Misty Fiords, Tracy Arm, and Glacier Bay, as well as at Anan Creek near Wrangell and Pack Creek in the Stan Price State Wildlife Sanctuary 30 miles south of Juneau. In August and September the banks of the Chilkoot River near Haines are another reliable viewing area. Bears hit the beach near Ketchikan to nibble kelp or dig clams. The least invasive way to watch animals, including bears, is to book a charter with a boat captain who knows where to find them grazing at low tide. For example, Alaska Discovery (907/780–6226), offers bear-viewing kayak trips at Admiralty Island.

At least 70 percent of a bear's diet is herbivorous, so if you can recognize bruin diet, you are a step ahead of the person elbowing you at the rail. In Glacier Bay, for example, bears dine on goat's beard, lady fern, various sedges, crowberry, beach pea, beach lovage, skunk cabbage, coastal strawberry, and cow parsnip.

Everyone clamors to see bears—but they are unpredictable beasts, and it's important to keep your distance. To master bear safety, read Dave Smith's *Backcountry Bear Basics.*

WHALES, SEALS, AND PORPOISES

About 1,000 humpback whales migrate annually to the Inside Passage and can be viewed April through September. Their breathing carries for miles, often revealing their presence. These huge, acrobatic mammals travel in pods of six to eight, taking shallow dives. They're commonly seen near Juneau and Admiralty Island, especially in passes and narrows along their migration routes. Whales come from Hawaii to feed on krill, capelin, herring, and sand lances.

Orcas (killer whales), minke whales, and porpoise may be sighted too. Orca pods follow salmon runs, so peak viewing periods are April through September. With an athleticism that defies their bulk, orcas are able to "spyhop," or pop their heads vertically out of the water without actually leaping. Both orcas and minkes can be seen in Glacier Bay, at Point Adolphus near Hoonah and in Frederick Sound. The Pacific white-sided dolphin is commonly spotted near Ketchikan. Both the Harbor porpoise and Dall's porpoise are common in Southeast Alaska. Harbor porpoises swim close to shore, but are shy and dive frequently. Dall's porpoises enjoy riding the bow waves of ferries. You can tell them apart by the way Dall's porpoises may jump or spin out of the water. (Harbor porpoises don't.)

Harbor seals may be seen year-round. Their pupping areas include Tracy Arm Fjord south of Juneau and Glacier Bay. When seals are pupping in May and June, waters near pupping haul-outs (reefs, beaches, and icebergs) are often closed to tour boats so that birthing and nursing continue undisturbed. Harbor seals are usually solitary, so if you see groups of "something" in the water spyhopping to look at you, you're probably seeing Steller sea lions. There are rookeries of Steller sea lions near Juneau, Gustavus, and Ketchikan. Near Outer Point on Douglas Island, I have had a seal trail my kayak like a heeling pup.

Remember, laws protect whales from ship traffic. Boats are not to approach closer than 100 yards. It's also forbidden to feed sea lions and other wild creatures. Substantial fines await vessel skippers or others found guilty of such practices.

BIRDS

My Juneau boss once remarked that bald eagles were so common they "weren't really wildlife." But most visitors can't get enough of these majestic beauties. Each bald eagle requires about a mile of shoreline for feeding; this means eagles perch in trees along the Inside Passage at regular intervals. They favor tall, dead trees as lookouts, but make do with wharf pilings and cupolas. The Alaska Chilkat Bald Eagle Preserve outside Haines is the best place to see eagles, but raptor centers in

Sitka and Juneau are also good bets. It's against the law to "chum" (cast fish scraps on the water) to lure eagles closer. Doing so will net the guilty party a heavy fine.

To the Haida, hunting birds was equivalent to a vision quest. Rufous hummingbirds, the crested Steller's Jay, cormorants, grebes, great blue herons, and Canada geese thrive along the Inside Passage. The Dusky Canada goose commutes year-round to Juneau's Mendenhall Wetlands. And ravens do their hokey-pokey near fast-food joints and supermarkets as they hunt for scraps.

ANIMAL SAFETY

Most wild animals have no desire to cross your path—but they should be warned of human presence so that you don't startle them. When hiking where visibility is limited by terrain or weather, **make noise.** Talk, sing, or whistle; if you have a trekking pole, attach bells to it and knock it against rocks. **Don't try to feed animals** or leave out food to attract them for close-up pictures.

BEARS

If you suddenly see a bear, it may perceive the place where you're standing as its right-of-way. Wave your arms to appear larger. Clap your hands. Speak to the bear. Never approach the bear and **never run away.** (Bears can easily outrun humans.) Stand your ground, or back up slowly. Bears, like most omnivores, consider anything fleeing as fair game. Never get between a sow and her cub. If you see a cub and not the sow, back away quietly. A brown bear's sense of smell is 100,000 times as acute as a human's, so don't piggyback a deer carcass. When camping, use airtight containers for food and cook away from your site. Don't bring edibles or anything that smells like food into your tent—fluoride toothpaste or oatmeal bars can attract a grizzly to nuzzle your sleeping bag. For more specifics, peruse the Alaska Department of Fish & Game Web site, www.adfg.state.ak.us.

MOOSE

Moose are totally unpredictable. If you run across one, it can retreat, its huge bulk quickly disappearing ghostlike in the brush—or it might advance at a trot to stomp you flat. Moose are rare in Southeast Alaska. Nevertheless, the Gustavus forelands have an estimated density of 3.8 moose per square kilometer, and sometimes moose outnumber humans two to one. If you do happen to see a moose on a trail, do not try to go around it. Wait 5 or 10 minutes to see

Mountain goats scrambling in Glacier Bay National Park.

if the dumb ungulate moves. If it stands its ground, retreat slowly and quietly. Like most protective moms, moose with calves will do their utmost to protect them from perceived danger.

ANTIQUITIES LAWS

After decades of unauthorized grave-robbing, Alaska takes its antiquities very seriously. The maximum fine is $250,000 and 10 years in jail.

Alaska's first antiquities laws went on the books in 1906. Rock hounds will be pleased to note, however, that it is permissible to collect small samples of ancient plant and invertebrate (snail, clam, etc.) fossils in most parts of the state, including the entire Inside Passage. No samples collected can be sold. On the other hand, unless you have a permit issued for scientific research, you may not collect or move any prehistoric or historic artifacts such as arrowheads, prospectors' boot soles on the Chilkoot Trail, old bottles, mining equipment, or human remains. Anyone stumbling upon dinosaur fossils is asked to notify authorities of their location. Petroglyphs (ancient markings on rock) are similarly protected.

BOATING

Waking up anchored in a quiet cove and watching porpoise chase sand eels or pilchards while you sip coffee is an unforgettable experience. Chartering a sailboat is one way to accomplish this goal. For charters with captains aboard, consult visitor centers for lists of recommended outfits.

Kayaks and power boats can be rented in most towns, with instruction gratis. If you're new to kayaking, the best way to gain confidence is to take a guided tour before going it alone. Try Doyle's Boat Rentals (877/442–4010) in Petersburg.

The quieter the craft you pilot, the more likely you are to spot wildlife before it spots you—and have the thrill of observing normal activity. If you've never experienced what John Muir called "the silvery level" (that is, water level), wonder awaits you. Guided tours on inflatable rafts can supply the heady excitement of rapids as well as plenty of scenery. Float trips are available out of most Inside Passage ports, and you can even paddle a traditional Tlingit canoe with Auk Ta Shaa Discovery (800/820–2628). Adventures Afloat (907/586–3312), 15 years in Juneau, offers personalized multi-day adventures on the 106-foot *Valkyrie* and 32-foot *High Roller.*

On the other hand, if speed and engine din are your cup of tea, board a jetboat. Breakaway Adventures offers jet boats out of Wrangell to the Stikine River, Anan Bear Observatory, and the Shakes and LeConte glaciers (888/385–2488). Alaska

Taking a dip in Metlakatla.

Vistas (866/874–3006) offers rafting trips of the Stikine River as well as guided kayak expeditions. Absolutely Alaskan/Yeshua Guided Tours offers jet boats in the Haines and Skagway areas (907/766–2334).

Sailors should note the "Spirit of Adventure-Around Admiralty" race, starting from Juneau's Auke Bay in mid-June. The 200-mile sailboat race is billed as the longest inland-water sailing race in the Pacific Northwest. The possibility of icebergs in Tracy Arm is just part of the fun.

CLIMATE

On a brief visit to Juneau in 1935, humorist Will Rogers was asked why he was buying two raincoats. "If I were staying longer, I'd buy three," Rogers replied.

The Inside Passage is a maritime "road" surrounded by rain forest. So equip yourself with a sturdy raincoat with attached hood or a folding umbrella. (Many cruise-ship lines distribute poncholike raingear—essentially giant trash bags with neck and arm holes—which offer scant protection.)

Down coats are unnecessary unless you chronically suffer from chilly extremities. Daytime summer temperatures range from 44°F to 85°F. Fifty-five degrees and cloudy is typical. The shoulder season is usually more blustery and chillier—hardy sightseers send home damp postcards logging the wind speed.

CLOTHING

Alaskans don shorts when the mercury reaches 55°F, but many visitors wrap up at that temperature. To best prepare for changing temperatures, dress in layers of synthetics with a fleece vest. Sidewalks tend to be uneven or nonexistent, so backless shoes, flimsy sandals, and high heels are risky. Sturdy lace-up walking shoes suffice for most exploration, except extended forays into the backcountry. Don't fret about your appearance; most Alaskans spurn high fashion.

Bound for a flightseeing tour featuring a glacier landing? Don a warm hat and gloves. Wear sunglasses to cut the glare from snow, ice, and water.

For fishing excursions, knee-high rubber boots are de rigueur, because you may need to wade to the boat. A hat with a brim all around helps to cut glare; it should have a chinstrap so that the wind can't kidnap it. Kayaking tour operators typically provide waterproof suits and boots as well as flotation vests.

Be prepared with a fleece hat, gloves, and scarf on day cruises, in mine tunnels, at outdoor theater performances, when whale- or bird-watching, golfing, beachcombing, dog sledding, or on float trips.

FESTIVALS AND ANNUAL EVENTS

Although most visitors tour the Inside Passage between May and September, special events and celebrations punctuate the entire year. Here is a sampling of some of the best.

JANUARY

The Alcan 200 Road Rally is a snow-machine race from the U.S./Canada border near Haines to Dezadeash Lake and back. The Polar Bear Dip on New Year's Day in Juneau brings out the hardy—and the shivering.

FEBRUARY

During the first weekend of this month, Wrangell's Tent City Days re-create some of the spirit of the 19th-century gold rushes with competitions like beard-growing and tall-tales contests. At the Shady Lady Fancy Dress Ball, women show off their décolletages.

MARCH

The Gold Medal Basketball Tournament brings teams from all over the state to Juneau. Teams of elders compete as if their lives depended on it.

APRIL

Mendenhall Golf Course, 10 miles from downtown, opens for play—with orange balls if there's snow cover. Juneau's Folk Festival offers musical headliners of all stripes. Ketchikan's all a-buzz during its Hummingbird Festival.

MAY

Petersburg's 2008 Little Norway Festival was its 50th annual. The festival celebrates Norwegian Constitution Day with a benign Viking raid. Look for Norwegian pastries and music as well as a halibut-filleting contest. Wrangell, Sitka, Ketchikan, and Petersburg all host salmon derbies. Haines guzzles regional microbrews at its Great Alaska Craftbeer & Homebrew Festival.

JUNE

Bicyclists drool over the Annual Kluane to Chilkat Bike Relay, from Haines Junction, Yukon Territory, to the Fort Seward parade grounds in Haines, Alaska. The course is 160 miles through spectacular Kluane Park and the Alaska Chilkat

The Children of All Nations Dancers wait to begin a performance in Juneau.

Bald Eagle Preserve. Juneau celebrates Gold Rush Days with logging and mining events. Sitka's Summer Music Festival attracts world-famous musicians.

JULY

Soapy Smith's Wake in Skagway toasts the infamous con man every July 8. Ketchikan stages its *Fish Pirate's Daughter* melodrama, and Prince of Wales Island puts on its Logging Show & Fair (www.princeofwalescoc.org). All Inside Passage towns whoop it up on the Fourth of July in a big way with parades, marching bands, and canoe races. Because of competition from the midnight sun, Juneau's Fourth of July fireworks display begins about 11:30 P.M. on July 3. However, the Midnight Sun phenomenon is much less evident along the Inside Passage than it is farther north.

AUGUST

Juneau holds its 60th annual Golden North Salmon Derby in 2006. There are significant cash prizes as well as prizes for catching tagged fish. The annual Blueberry Arts Festival in Ketchikan includes a pie-eating contest. Haines hosts the annual Southeast Alaska State Fair, showcasing local activities with events like a logging show and a fiddle contest.

SEPTEMBER

The Klondike Road Relay, a 110-mile race, kicks off in Skagway and ends in Whitehorse. Sitka holds its Labor Day Weekend Mudball Classic Softball Tournament.

OCTOBER

Sitka honors Alaska Day on the 18th, the anniversary of formal ceremonies marking the 1867 purchase of Alaska from Russia. Festivities continue for several days and include a costume ball. Petersburg's Gallery Walk is part of a month of special events.

NOVEMBER

Haines toasts its eagles with the Alaska Bald Eagle Festival (www.baldeaglefest. org). Sitka begins Holiday Fest, which continues through January.

DECEMBER

Sitka launches its Christmas Boat Parade. Juneau's Gallery Walk highlights visiting and resident artists. Haines ushers in the winter holidays with a Snow Dragon Parade.

FISHING

Along the Inside Passage there's little "combat fishing"—fishing shoulder-to-shoulder with a hundred others. Here you can charter a vessel to take you away from all that, to show you the captain's favorite reefs or halibut holes.

But don't expect to hook onto a big one on your first cast. By interviewing fishermen, the Alaska Department of Fish & Game keeps a running total of the hours an average marine boat angler needed to land each species. For example, a five-year average for catching coho salmon in the Juneau area is four hours.

Runs occur during different weeks in different parts of the Inside Passage. The first spring runs are herring and hooligan, caught in dip nets. They're delectable eating deep fried, served on ferns. In Sitka, angle for smelt (hooligan) in May and early June from the steel bridge over the Taiya River, at milepost 5.7 on the Dyea Road.

In general, kings (the largest salmon and the state fish) spawn in spring and finish by mid-summer; sockeye, chum, and pink follow the king run; acrobatic silvers head for shore in August and September. For availability of halibut, Dolly Varden, rockfish, and other species, consult a personable guide.

For an adventure to boast about, consider a fishing "escape" in a remote location, such as Icy Strait Point. The original settlement here was a salmon cannery built in 1912. The cannery has been restored and modified to include a fishing history museum, a restaurant, lounge, and shops. Salmon and halibut are the catch here. Icy Point is 20 minutes by air from Juneau. For details, contact Icy Strait Lodge (866/645–3636).

For fishing around the capital or to learn bag and possession limits, visit http://juneaualaska.com/fishing, or call the Division of Sport Fish (907/465–4270) or the Fishing Hotline (907/465–4116).

Nonresident sport-fishing licenses and king salmon stamps ($10 extra) are sold at many marine supply outlets and even some drugstores. To purchase a license online, go to www.admin.adfg.state.ak.us/license. Licenses are not required for children under 16.

How big is a trophy? The king salmon averages 15 to 50 pounds; 50 pounds or over is considered a trophy. A "barn door" halibut is anything over 100 pounds—and always female. A rainbow trout 10 pounds or more, grayling 3 pounds, and red salmon 12 pounds are also trophy. Believe me, a fish of 20 pounds can put up a memorable struggle; you'll be glad your biceps are buff if you hook into one.

During summer months, most towns hold fishing derbies with impressive cash prizes; for an extra fillip to your fishing trip, enter a contest such as Wrangell's King Salmon Derby (mid-May to mid-June). The top prize is $6,000.

FLIGHTSEEING

If you enjoy flying low enough to see swans on their nests, bush planes offer an exhilarating look at the landscape. Operators usually have scheduled tour itineraries, but may also be willing to take you wherever you wish to go. Be aware, however, that weather fronts can quickly reduce visibility and change everyone's plans.

TEMSCO Helicopters (877/789–9501) developed Alaska's first glacier helicopter tour in 1983. They lift off at Wrangell, Juneau, and Skagway. All tours include narration, and most are in A-star turbine helicopters known for their quiet ride and unobstructed views from every seat.

From Wrangell, one TEMSCO tour whisks you up the Stikine River and gives a good look at the tidewater LeConte Glacier. From Skagway, the Valley of the Glaciers flight lands at the base of a glacier. This flight is a more intimate experience than passing over an ice field; you'll get up close and personal with canyons and dramatic peaks. From Juneau, one popular trip includes views of the Juneau Ice Field and gives you 20 to 25 minutes with a mountaineering guide on the glacier surface. (Boots with good traction are provided.) Another Juneau option pairs a flight with a landing at a dog camp to try mushing—driving or riding in the sled.

In addition to TEMSCO, Wings of Alaska, L.A.B. Flying Service, Promech Air, Haines Airways, and other fly-boys serve the Inside Passage.

Note: Due to weight and balance restrictions, passengers weighing 250 pounds or more are sometimes charged an additional half-fare to reserve helicopter space.

FOOD

Although fresh seafood is ubiquitous in summer, few people come to the Inside Passage for the cuisine. Hamburgers and steaks are common. Adventure here lies not in the dining room but in gliding past icebergs close enough to hear them drip.

Alaska has scant agriculture, so many basic ingredients—produce, corn, citrus fruit, beef, free-range chicken—must be flown or barged in. So ask about the catch of the day and hope it won't be overcooked. On the other hand, North Slope reindeer, Haines herbs, Delta Junction buffalo, Kachemak Bay mussels, or Matanuska Valley cabbage and carrots may be in season; look for these on local menus or inquire. If you're preparing for an alfresco meal, stop by a local bakery, market, or takeout for anything from bright green seaweed salad to cranberry muffins. Fried chicken, egg rolls, sushi, a pass at the salad bar, and a brace of fresh macaroons make a tempting lunch—often less expensive than a restaurant one. Find a park bench and enjoy the sunshine. Kiosks crowd Juneau's downtown sidewalks during the high season, serving everything from pork adobo to fry bread.

Dining suggestions appear with each town's listing. Symbols show the cost you may expect:

Prices for a main course at dinner (or equivalent)	
$	less than $10
$$	$10 to $20
$$$	$20 to $30
$$$$	over $40

GETTING AROUND

Towns along the Inside Passage are in some ways isolated, as most lack highway and rail infrastructure. In fact, there is only one mile of road for every 44 square miles of land, and only 32 percent of that road is paved.

However, the Alaska Marine Highway, the state's ferry system, links the communities of the Inside Passage via its regular 1,048-mile circuit. The "Big Blue Canoes" sail from Bellingham, Washington, to Skagway. The breathtaking scenery along this circuit earned it a National Scenic Byway designation in 2002. Reservations should be confirmed six months in advance (ferryalaska. com; 800/642–0066). Some visitors drive to Skagway or Haines and get aboard the ferry there. Ferries have excellent dining rooms, with hot beverages generally available at all times. Locals tend to take no-frills trips, camping on deck, but there are also cabins available. AMH now has a couple of faster ferries. Be sure to inquire about whether you're getting the "milk run" or the speedier craft.

The most-visited Inside Passage towns have tours tracing a specified route, and for the price of a ticket you can get off and reboard at any of their regular stops in your own good time. On the other hand, if you draw up a list of preferred destinations in advance, a taxi driver can customize your tour. (Contact the local chamber of commerce or visitors bureau for taxi recommendations.) Bicycle rentals are generally available, but bike paths may be skimpy, under construction, or repurposed, unpaved logging roads.

Most cruise-ship lines and tour operators own their own sightseeing buses, which will be omnipresent at cruise-ship docks. Gray Line of Alaska (800/544–2206) offers coach tours and connections to such activities as whale-watching and Mendenhall River float trips out of Juneau and a Totem Bight tour out of Ketchikan. If you have not made up your mind about excursions before arriving, spontaneous decisions may be made on the spot. In fact, locals are not allowed on some excursions, in order to keep all seats for tourists.

Then there are the bush flights or air taxis. It could be as simple as a 20-minute flight with just you, a companion, the pilot, and three seats of groceries. But caveat emptor: flight services tend to hire summer-season pilots who are unused to Alaskan flight conditions. Before buying a ticket, it pays to ask the pilot about how long he or she's been flying in the area, so you can pick someone with local experience.

GOLD PANNING

Prospectors have investigated nearly every water course in Alaska for gold. And many waterways will yield that precious metal—albeit in infinitesimal flakes. Gold panning and other recreational mining activities are permitted on most public lands and in rivers classified "wild," but be sure to contact parkland managers and don't trespass on property posted "private." If panning is a must-try on your list, check with the local visitor center for creeks where this activity is allowed.

At its most basic, panning is sloshing water, dirt, and gravel around in large pie plates. Gold is very heavy, so as you slosh away the lighter dirt and gravel the shiny precious metal will be left behind in your pan. First scoop the gravel you want to prospect into your pan. Then shake the pan in a left-to-right motion under water. Lighter materials will be washed away.

Alaska Travel Adventures (800/791–2673 outside Alaska; 800/478–0052 inside Alaska; www.alaskaadventures.com) offers gold panning in Juneau. During Juneau's A-J Mine/Gastineau Mill tour (907/463–3900) you will have a chance to pan for gold (guaranteed in every pan). In Juneau, Goldbelt Tours also offers gold panning with guaranteed gold in every pan (907/586–8687). Hobbyist panners with personal sluice boxes pan for free in Juneau's Gold Creek at Cope Park. To study up on panning methods in advance, check the Web site of The New 49'ers Club, www.goldgold.com.

GREEN TRAVEL: BIKE TOURS

Traveling on two wheels is an efficient way to plot your own adventure tour. It enables you to explore dirt roads with little motorized traffic for competition.

Sockeye Cycle maintains full-service shops with repairs and rentals in both Haines (24 Portage St.; 907/766–2869) and Skagway (381 5th Ave.; 907/983–2851). With 20 years experience under their belts, they wheel out five different escorted tours in Haines. These include a Cannery Cove tour, a Chilkat Pass tour, and a Porcupine Gold tour. In Skagway, there are four guided choices, including the Klondike Rainforest tour and—the best of two transportation worlds—the White Pass train and Bike combo.

In the capital, Cycle Alaska Juneau (3172 Pioneer Ave., 907/723–1876) offers three guided excursions: Zip & Bike, Bike & Brew, and Sky & Sea. Zip & Bike connects with a zipline tour at Eaglecrest and then takes in the sights at the North Douglas Boat Ramp. Bike & Brew starts at Chapel by the Lake, hits the west and east sides of Mendenhall, and then researches the foam at Alaskan Brewing. Sky & Sea heads to the beach and forest at False Outer Point and returns to downtown.

In Wrangell, Klondike Bikes (502 Wrangell Ave., 907/874–2453) offers repairs and rentals. Owner Dave Sweat says many of his customers come to town for the weeklong Fourth of July spectacular, which includes fireworks, a gravity car race, and a logging show. Sweat distributes free advice for self-guided bikers, as well as forest service maps of unpaved logging roads around Wrangell.

To keep Southeast what it is, follow these low-impact practices: 1) Don't leave litter or food behind. 2) Don't widen trails. 3) Do not disturb vegetation or wildlife

LODGING AND CAMPING

Lodging of all sorts is available along the Inside Passage—whether you're looking for a barebones cabin, a dormitory-type hostel, or all the bells and whistles like cable modem access and an in-room whirlpool tub.

In Skagway, Juneau, and Haines, look for rooms in historic buildings. (In Haines, for example, you can stay at Hotel Halsingland, the former Fort William H. Seward.) There's a good sprinkling of fishing lodges too, in places like Prince of Wales Island and Baranof Island. Don't count on chains like Motel 8, but note that rates drop significantly during off-season, sometimes 25 percent or more.

For bed-and-breakfasts, vacation homes, cabins, and lodges throughout the Southeast, get in touch with Alaska Travelers Accommodations (800/928–3308). If you want a kitchenette, you may need to make reservations months in advance. (Wilderness cabins are equipped with kitchens, but bring your own camping stove and heating fuel.) Ketchikan Reservation Service (800/987–5337; 907/247–5337, phone-fax) handles reservations in the Ketchikan area.

The U.S. Forest Service rents rustic cabins sleeping 6 to 16, for $35 a night. Call the National Recreation Reservation Service at 877/444–6777. Some cabins are accessed via hiking trails; others require kayak, boat, or pontoon-equipped bush plane access. State parks also offer cabins at $25 a night; call 907/465–4563 or log on to www.dnr.state.ak.us/parks/index.htm.

Most of the larger Inside Passage towns have RV parks and campgrounds, including Juneau, Wrangell, Petersburg, Sitka, and Skagway. There are campsites at state parks and national parks in the Haines area. For low-tech travelers exploring with knapsack in the European style, Ketchikan and Sitka both have hostels affiliated with Hostelling International (202/783–6161); other towns, including Juneau, Petersburg, and Skagway, have privately owned hostels.

SHOPPING TIPS

Remember the old saw about "How do porcupines mate? Carefully."? The same applies to shopping. There are a lot of made-in-China fakes in Alaska. If you wish to purchase Native-made art or craft, make sure it comes with a certification tag or ask for a guarantee penned on your sales slip. Legitimate galleries create information sheets about each artist; request one to insure the origin of your purchase. The Silver Hand tag assures authenticity, with the words "Native Handicraft from Alaska." The name of the artist may be penned in. The Made in Alaska emblem guarantees the piece was made in the state—but not necessarily by a Native (www.dced.state.ak.us/dca/mia/home.htm).

For details, read the brochure *Alaskan Native Art* put out by the Alaska Attorney General's Office and the Alaska State Council on the Arts (888-278-7424; www.educ.state.ak.us/aksca/).

Alaska's terrain can be unforgiving. **Don't take the risks lightly.** Every year people drown, become disoriented and lost, suffer from hypothermia, or fall to their deaths. Check with the Forest Service when planning a hiking, camping, canoeing, or kayaking outing. Obtain trail maps, permits, and weather reports before heading out. Ask about bear density—and recent bear sightings. Take sufficient clothing, food, and water. If your knees and ankles wobble a bit, use trekking poles. Carry a VHF hand-held radio on extended kayak trips. Leave a detailed float or flight plan behind so someone will alert search and rescue (SAR) authorities if you're late returning. If the weather looks at all threatening, don't push ahead. And don't rely on cell phones, as they may not work in remote areas.

Do your best to **prevent hypothermia.** Hypothermia is a decrease in the body's core temperature to a level at which normal physical and mental functions are impaired. Severe hypothermia can be fatal. Avoid it by wearing layers of clothing (including a windbreaker), changing wet clothing for dry, keeping hydrated, and avoiding fatigue. Warning symptoms include shivering, goose bumps, and accelerated heartbeat, followed by stumbling and slurred speech. Don't drink alcohol, as this speeds heat loss.

Giardia, an intestinal parasite that can cause cramps and diarrhea, is common in Alaskan streams and rivers. **Boil, filter, or chemically treat all water you use.**

When kayaking, fishing, canoeing, or traveling in a small boat, **wear a life jacket.** Keep in mind that ocean swells, opposing currents, rapids, and boat wakes can sink small craft. Alaskan waters are extremely cold; death is almost certain within 15 minutes of immersion. Consult a tide book before setting out. (Tide tables for Juneau, Ketchikan, and Sitka are printed in PDC's Southeast Alaska phone book.)

Watch your footing. Many trails are narrow, with steep drop-offs, unstable footing, fractured rock, mossy logs, roots, or slippery slate. It's very easy to sprain an ankle and be stranded. Consider carrying a police whistle to signal for help.

If you have been dropped off at a remote site by a bush plane, keep in mind that weather and visibility can delay scheduled pickups.

TIME

Southeast Alaska is on Alaska Time, one hour earlier than Pacific Time.

TRAVELING WITH KIDS

Kid Stuff sections within each chapter offer specific activities.

In Ketchikan, fearless kids will enjoy the chills and thrills offered by Alaska Canopy Adventures (907/225–5503). ACA's zip-line courses include suspension bridges, sky bridges, tree platforms up to 135 feet above the forest floor. Children under 5 years or 50 pounds cannot use zip lines. Weight limitation for others is 250 pounds. Minors must be accompanied by a parent.

Many cruise lines host activities for children or grandchildren: Carnival has scheduled onboard programs for ages 2 through 14 and special shore excursions for teens.

Celebrity offers activities for kids 3 to 17. Crystal has supervised children's programs.

Holland America offers scheduled supervised programs for ages 5 to 12. Norwegian has activities on ship and in port for kids 2 to 17, including dancing, arts and crafts, treasure hunts, costume making, and games. Princess offers activities involving science, wildlife and conservation plus big screen TVs, for ages 3 to 17. Royal Caribbean has ice-skating rinks and rock-climbing walls on some ships. Most lines offer babysitting, for a fee.

USEFUL CONTACTS

- **All emergencies:** 911.
- **Area code for the entire state of Alaska:** 907.
- **Fish and Game licensing:** 907/465–2376.
- **Time and temperature:** 907/586–3185 (for Juneau) or www.inalaska.com/alaska/weather (entire state).
- **U.S. Coast Guard:** 800/478–5555 for Maritime Search and Rescue; 800/478–6381 for boating registration.
- **U.S. Customs:** 907/586–7211; www.customs.gov.
- **Weather in Alaska:** 800/472–0391 (National Weather Service).

CRUISE LINES

- **American Safari Cruises:** 888/862–8881; www.amsafari.com.
- **American West Steamboat Company:** 800/434–1232; www.columbiariver cruise.com.
- **Carnival Cruise Lines:** 800/227–6482; www.carnival.com.
- **Celebrity Cruises:** 800/437–3111; www.celebrity.com.

Cruise ships ease into Juneau's Gastineau Channel.

- **Clipper Cruise Line:** 800/325–0010; www.clippercruise.com.
- **Cruise West:** 800/888–9378; www.cruisewest.com.
- **Crystal Cruises:** 800/820–6663; www.crystalcruises.com.
- **Glacier Bay Cruise Line:** 800/451–5952; www.glacierbaytours.com.
- **Holland America Westours**: 877/724–5425; www.hollandamerica.com.
- **Linblad Expeditions:** 800/397–3348; www.expeditions.com.
- **Majestic America Line:** 800/434–1232; www.majesticamericaline.com.
- **Norwegian Cruise Lines:** 800/327–7030; www.ncl.com.
- **Princess Cruises:** 800/774–6237; www.princess.com.
- **Radisson Seven Seas Cruises:** 877/505–5370; www.rssc.com.
- **Royal Caribbean Cruise Line:** 800/327–6700; www.royalcaribbean.com.

TRANSPORTATION

- **Alaska Airlines:** 800/252–7522; www.alaskaair.com.
- **Alaska Fjordlines:** 800/320–0146; www.alaskafjordlines.com; passenger-only ferry service between Haines, Juneau, and Skagway from late May through August.
- **Alaska Marine Highway Reservations:** 800/642–0066; TDD, 800/764–3779; www.alaska.gov/ferry.
- **Alaska Rent-A-Car:** 800/662–0007; www.akcarrental.com. Ketchikan only.
- **Budget Rent A Car**: 800/527–0700; www.budget.com. Juneau only.
- **Chilkat Cruises:** 907/766–2100; www.chilkatcruises.com; ferry service between Haines and Skagway from May through September.
- **ERA Helicopters,** Juneau, Anchorage: 907/586–2030.
- **Fjord Flying Service,** Gustavus: 907/697–2377.
- **Harris Aircraft Services Inc.,** Sitka: 907/966–3050.
- **Inter-Island Ferry Authority,** Petersburg, Wrangell, Prince of Wales: 866/308–4848.
- **Ketchikan Air:** 907/225–4641.
- **Kupreanof Flying Service:** 907/772–3396; www.kupreanof.com.
- **L.A.B. Flying Service Inc.:** 907/766–2222; www.labflying.com.
- **Pacific Wing Air Charters,** Petersburg: 907/772–4258.
- **Promech Air,** Ketchikan: 907/225–3845; www.promechair.com.
- **Sunrise Aviation,** Wrangell: 907/874–2311; www.sunriseflights.com.
- **Ward Air Inc.,** Juneau: 907/789–9150.
- **Wings of Alaska Airlines:** 907/789–0790; www.wingsofalaska.com.
- **Yakutat Coastal Airlines:** 907/784–3831.

- **Alaska Department of Fish & Game, Division of Wildlife Conservation:** www.wildlifenews.alaska.gov.
- **Alaska Marine Highway:** 800/642–0066; www.FerryAlaska.com.
- **Alaska Public Lands Information Center,** Ketchikan: 907/228–6214; www.nps.gov/aplic/.
- **Alaska Relay** (telecommunications relay service for deaf, hard of hearing, and speech disabled): TTY 800/770–8973.
- **Alaska Scenic Byways Program:** 907/465–8769; www.alaska.gov/scenic.
- **Alaska Travel Industry Information:** www.travelalaska.com.
- **Challenge Alaska:** 907/344–7399; www.challengealaska.org; information about access for people with disabilities.
- **Glacier Bay National Park Service:** 907/697–2230; www.nps.gov/glac/.
- **Haines Convention & Visitors Bureau**: 800/458–3579; www.haines.ak.us/.
- **Juneau Convention & Visitors Bureau:** 888/581–2201; www.traveljuneau.com.
- **JuneauAlaska.com:** www.juneaualaska.com; online visitor guide supported by the *Juneau Empire* newspaper.
- **Ketchikan Ranger District/Misty Fiords National Monument:** 907/225–2148; www.fs.fed.us/r10/tongass/districts/ketchikan/ktnmisty.
- **Ketchikan Visitors Bureau:** 907/225–6166; www.visit-ketchikan.com.
- **Klondike Gold Rush National Historical Park Visitor Center,** Skagway: 907/983-2921; www.nps.gov/klgo/.
- **Petersburg Visitor Information Center:** 907/772–4636 or 866/484–4700; www.petersburg.org.
- **Sitka Convention & Visitors Bureau:** 907/747–5940; www.sitka.org.
- **Skagway Convention & Visitors Bureau:** 907/983–2854; www.skagway.com.
- **Southeast Alaska Tourism Council**: 907/586–5777; www.alaskainfo.org.
- **Tongass National Forest:** 907/225-3101; www.fs.fed.us/r10/tongass/.
- **Wrangell Visitor Information:** 907/874–3901 or 800/367–9745; www.wrangell.com or www.wrangellchamber.org.

RECOMMENDED READING

Clifford, Howard, *The Skagway Story,* 2003. Colorful characters and amusing anecdotes abound in this well-researched portrait of a city and its early history.

Demerjian, Bonnie. *Roll On! Discovering the Wild Stikine River,* 2006. Demerjian's lively text covers everything from geologic formation to riverboats, gold rushes, wild life, development, and preservation.

Drucker, Philip, *Cultures of the North Pacific Coast,* 1965. A comprehensive anthropological and sociological review of the culture of the Northwest Coast, including topics such as warfare and shamanism.

Emmons, George, and Frederica de Laguna, *The Tlingit Indians,* 1991. An ethnography with historical depth presented in chronological order.

Ferguson, Judy, *Alaska's First People: Traveling with Grampa*, 2007. This artful children's book lets you in on the tastes, sights, sounds, and smells of places like Metlakatla and Point Hope.

Mergler, Wayne, Editor, *The Last New Land: Stories of Alaska, Past and Present,* 1996. This anthology is a bedside treasure, offering traditional legends as well as contemporary poems, stories, and essays. Jack London rubs shoulders with Ernie Pyle, Dana Stabenow, and Spike Walker.

Moessner, Victoria Joan, Translator and Editor, *The First Russian Voyage around the World: The Journal of Hermann Ludwig von Lowenstern, 1803–1806,* 2003. Read about exploration from the horse's mouth. Von Lowenstern served as fourth officer on the lead ship *Nadezhda.*

Muir, John. Introduction by Edward Hoagland, *Travels in Alaska,* 2002 (Modern Library). Muir made the first of many trips to Alaska in 1879. *Travels in Alaska* originally appeared in 1915, the year after his death. His legacy is literary as well as conservationist; his descriptions of Wrangell, Sum Dum Bay, Stickeen Glacier. and many other Southeast locations simply cannot be bettered.

O'Clair, Rita, Robert H. Armstrong, and Richard Carstensen, *The Nature of Southeast Alaska,* 1997. The authors, all Juneau residents expert in their fields, serve forth facts about plants and animals illustrated with detailed pen-and-ink drawings.

Dwarf dogwood (*Cornus canadensis*) in bloom.

Pratt, Verna E., *Field Guide to Alaskan Wildflowers,* 1989. Photos, maps, and a glossary of leaf and blossom shapes aid you in identifying flowering botanicals.

Stowell, Harold H., *Geology of Southeast Alaska: Rock and Ice in Motion,* 2005. Text and illustrations elucidate the powerful forces at work behind scenes in Southeast, with particular emphasis on Sitka, Juneau, and Glacier Bay.

Wilson, Graham, *The Klondike Gold Rush: Photographs from 1896–1899,* 1997. Archival images illustrate the "last great adventure" and the life of the average stampeder.

Wynne, Kate, *Guide to Marine Mammals of Alaska,* 2006. Printed on water-resistant stock, this identification guide to 30 species is handy at sea or on shore.

INDEX

Many sites and attractions listed below are followed by an abbreviation indicating the town/island/preserve in which each is found: (GBNP)=Glacier Bay National Park and Preserve; (H)=Haines; (J)=Juneau; (K)=Ketchikan; (MFNM)=Misty Fiords National Monument; (P)=Petersburg; (POW)=Prince of Wales Island; (Sit)=Sitka; (Sk)=Skagway; (TNF)=Tongass National Forest; (W)=Wrangell.

A

Aak'w Village site (J)–100

Absolutely Alaskan tours–185

accessibility–80 (P), 105 (J), 173 (Sit), 199, TTY 198

accommodations. See Alaska Travelers Accommodations, bed & breakfast accommodations, cabin reservations, food, hostels, lodging, RV parks

Admiralty Island–86, 110

Admiralty Island National Monument–photo 108-109, 112, 181

Adventure Bound cruises–110

Adventure Kart Expedition (K)–43

Adventures Afloat (J)–184

Air Excursions–160

air travel–38, 112, 128, 136, 156, 160, 190, 198

A-J Mine/Gastineau Mill Enterprises tour (J)–104, 192

Alaska Airlines–160, 198

Alaska area code–196

Alaska Backcountry Outfitters (H)–137

Alaska Bald Eagle Festival (H)–138, 188

Alaska Canopy Adventures–102

Alaska Chilkat Bald Eagle Preserve (H)–135, 138, 143, photo 145, 148, 181

Alaska Charters & Adventures (W)–65

Alaska Day–29, 188

Alaska Department of Fish and Game–73, 182, 189, contact information 199

Alaska Discovery (bear-viewing kayak trips)–180

Alaska Eagle Arts (K)–49

Alaska Fish House (K)–48

Alaska Fjordlines (H, J, Sk)–198

Alaska Fly-N-Fish (J)–112

Alaska Gastineau gold mine (J)–94

Alaska Genealogy Resource Guide (Alaska State Library)–97

Alaska Hummingbird Festival (K)–186

Alaska Indian Arts (H)–135, 137, 142

Alaska-Juneau (A-J) gold mine (J)–94, 97, 98

Alaska Lumber and Pulp Company–170

Alaska Marine Highway ferry system–130, 140, 191, contact information 198, 199

Alaska Marine Highway Reservations–198

Alaska Mountain Guides & International Wilderness Leadership School (H)–148

Alaska Native Art (brochure)–194

Alaska Native Claims Settlement Act–29, 171

Alaska Nature Tours (H)–map 137

Alaska Peak & Seas (W)–65

Alaska Public Lands Information Center (K)–199

Alaska Purchase, 1867–28, 54, 134, 168, 170, 188

Alaska Raptor Center (Sit)–171

Alaska Relay (TTY)–198

Alaska Rent-A-Car (K)–198

Alaska Scenic Byways Program–199

Alaska Seafood Marketing Institute (J)–102

Alaska Seaplane Service–112

Alaska Sightseeing/Cruise West–58, 157

Alaska State Archives (J)–97

Alaska State Capitol (J)–94-95

Alaska State Library (J)–97

Alaska State Museum (J)–100

Alaska State Troopers (H)–149

Alaska Time–195

Alaska Travel Adventures–47, 105, 192

Alaska Travel Industry Information–199

Alaska Travelers Accommodations–194

Alaska Vistas–185

Alaska Waters jet boat tour company (W)–66

Alaska Zipline Adventures (J)–102

Alaskan Chef's Table (K)–49

Alaskan Fudge Company (J)–101

Alaskan Hotel & Bar (J)–94

Alaska's First People: Traveling with Grampa (Ferguson)–200

Alcan 200 Road Rally–186

Aleut people–166

Aleutian Islands–28

American Bald Eagle Foundation (H)–146

American Safari Cruises–196

American West Steamboat Company–196

Anan Creek Bear Observatory–65, 180

ancestors, tracing Gold Rush–97

Anchorage, Alaska–21

Angoon–map 11

animal safety–180, 182-183

animal watching–180-183

Annahootz Alaskan Adventures (Sit)–178

Annette Island–23, 47

antiquities laws–183

archaeology–21, 30, 83

Archangel Michael (Old Sitka)–162

Arctic Brotherhood Hall (Sk)–127-128

area code, Alaska–196

Armstrong, Robert–200

art galleries–43

Arthur, Big Dolly–40

Astor, John Jacob–167

at.oow–178

Auk Ta Shaa Discovery–184

Auk Tlingit–83

B

Bald Eagle Foundation (H)–146

bald eagles–17, 29, 65, 74, 101, 133, 135, 138, 143, photos 144-145, 147, 149, 171

Bar Point Basin marina (K)–41

Baranof, Alexander (Aleksandr)–9, 24, 25-26, 162, 166

Baranof Island–162

Barley, H. C.–121

Barnett, H. G.–22

Bartlett Cove (GBNP)–156, 161

Bartlett Cove Trail (GBNP)–160

Basin Road (J)–87, 105

baskets, Native–44, 62, 113, 168

Battery Point Trail (H)–map 137

Battle of Sitka, 1804–26, 176

Bayview Trading Company–178

Bealer, Eric–179

bear watching, 65, 178, 180, 195

Beardslee Islands (GBNP)–161

bears–30 (K) ,47 (MFNM), 62-63, 66(W), 110 (J), 130 (Sk), 178 (Sit)

bears, prehistoric remains of–62

Beartrack Mercantile–156

Beartrack River (GBNP)–11

Bear-up-the-Mountain Totem (W)–64

Beasley, Michael–95

beaver–100, 177

Beaver Clan House (Saxman Village)–45

bed & breakfast accommodations–194

Behm Canal (K)–42

Belcher, Commander Edward–24

Bella Coola people–19

Bellingham, Washington–140, 191

Ben Moore House (Sk)–127

"bergy seltzer"–155

Bering Sea Crab Fishermens' Tour–46

Berner's Bay (J)–86

Best of Ketchikan Land & Sea Tour–42

bike trails, races, rentals, tours–66, 186, 188, 192, 193

Billings, Captain Joseph–24

Birch Boy Products–66-67

Birch Street Boardwalk (P)–74

birch syrup–66

bird watching–181-182

birds–14, 43, 66, 70, 76, 93, 101, 104, 149, 171, 181-182

Black, Martha–122

Blind River Rapids Trail (P)–80

Bloodgood, C.D.–168

Blue Jacket Creek archeological site–22

Blueberry Arts Festival (K)–30, 43, 188

boating–42 (MFNM), 61 (W), 184-185

Bojer-Wikan Fisherman's Memorial Park (P)–map 71, 74

Book of the Tongass, The (Alaback)–138

Bowhay, Cindy and Steve–105

Boysen, Carson, artist–74

Brackett's Trading Post (Sk)–123

Brady, Governor John Green–170

Brady Icefield (GBNP)–map 154, 160

Breakaway Adventures (W)–66, 184

Breece, Hannah–92

Bridal Veil Falls (Sk)–129

British Columbia–2, 50

Brown, William–98

bubble-net feeding–75

Budget Rent A Car (J)–198

Bureau of Indian Affairs (BIA)–20-21, 57

bus travel–192

Buschmann, Peter–69, 74

bush planes–192, 195

button blanket–176

C

cabin reservations–80, 177, 194

California Gold Rush–168

camping–131, 156, 161, 193-194

Canada–map 11, 19, 115, 126

Canadian customs (H)–149

canneries–35, 43 (K), 56 (W), 69 (P), 134, 142 (H), 189

Cannery Cove bike tour–193

cannery museum (H)–142

Cape Decision lighthouse–93

Cape Fairweather–map 11

Cape Fox Lodge (K)–40, 48-49

Cape Fox Tours (K)–43

Cape Spencer lighthouse–93

car rental–198

Carcross, Yukon Territory–map 11, 115

Carmack, George–118

Carnival Cruise Lines–196

Carstensen, Richard–200

Cassiar gold rush, British Columbia–50, 56

Castle Hill (Sit)–166, 172

Cathedral of the Archangel Michael (Sit)–172, 178

Cathedral Peaks (H)–133, photo 139

caves–30, 47

cedar trees–17, 38, 59

Celebrity Cruises–196

Centennial Exhibition, Philadelphia, 1876–59

Centennial Hall/Visitor Center (J)

Challenge Alaska–199

Chatham–25

Chez Alaska Cooking School–102

Chichagof Wilderness–178

Chicken Ridge (J)–95

Chief Johnson Totem (K)–39, 41

Chief Kadashan–56

Chief Kowee of the Auk Tlingit–88

Chief Kyan Totem (K)–38, 40, 41

Chief Shakes Hot Springs (W)–57, 66

Chief Shakes house (W)–54

Chief Shakes Island (W)–50, 63

Chief Shakes VII–58

Chief Shakes VI–64

Chief Toyatte–55

Chiefs of the Sea and Sky (Ehrlich)–23, 35

Chihuly, Dale, glass artist–131

children, traveling with–196

children's activities. See Kid Stuff

Chilkat–25

Chilkat blankets–128, 142, 147, 165, 176

Chilkat Cruises (H, S)–198

Chilkat Dancers Storytelling Theater –143

Chilkat Guides–148

Chilkat Pass bike tour–193

Chilkat River–148

Chilkat State Park (H)–140

Chilkat Tribal House (H)–.
See Fort William Seward

Chilkat Valley (H)–138

Chilkoot Lake State
Recreation Site (H)–133,
140

Chilkoot Pass–128

Chilkoot Pass Trail–117,
map 119, 122, 126, 131,
183

Chilkoot Tlingit–128

Chinook Trading
Language–118

Christmas Boat Parade
(Sit)–189

Christmas events–189

clan crests–22, 59

Clarence Strait–10, 34

Clausen Memorial Museum
(P)–74

climate–17, 18, 19, 185, 195,
196

Clipper Cruise Lines–198

clothing–131, 185, 195

Clover, Richardson–10

Coastal Wilderness
Adventures (Sit)–178

Colyer, Vincent–55

commercial fishing–77, 92,
102

conservation–38, 143, 146

Cook, Captain James–22,
59, 141

Copper River Ahtna–162

Corrington Museum of
Alaskan History (Sk)–131

cottonwood trees–18, 104

Council of the Clans, The,
modern totems (K)–40

crab catch–46, 73

Craig–21

Creek Street (K)–39

Creek Street Boardwalk
(K)–photo, 31, map,
32, 39

Crescent Harbor (Sit)–162,
164, map

Cross Sound Express
(GBNP)–160

crows–147

cruise lines, cruise ships–44,
58, 81, 83, 112, 115, 130,
137, 157, 160, 172, 180,
196, 198

Cruise Ship Terminal Dock
(J)–92

Cruise West–198

cruises, early Inside
Passage–44

Crystal Cruises–198

Crystal Lake Fish Hatchery
(P)–78

Crystal Mountain (P)–69

Cubby Hole, The (P)–77

Cultures of the North Pacific
Coast (Drucker)–200

Curtis, Asahel–121

Cycle Alaska Juneau–193

D

Dalton, Jack–134

Dalton City, set of Disney
movie White Fang
(H)–143

Dalton Trail–134

Darth Vader–135

Davidson Glacier (H)–135

Davis, Francis Brooks,
painter–95

Davis, J. Montgomery–95

Davis, Jefferson–56, 170

Dawson City, Yukon
Territory–115

Days of Adventure, Dreams of
Gold film (Sk)–127

Days of '98 Show (Sk)–128

de la Bodega y Quadra, Juan
Francisco–34

de Laguna, Frederica–200

de Roquefeuil, Camille–24

deer, Sitka black-tailed–17,
30, 47, 74, 83, 177

Deer Mountain Tribal
Hatchery and Eagle
Center (K)–40

Demerjian, Bonnie–200

Denver Glacier–128

Devil's Club–17, 87, 177

Dewey Lakes Trail (Sk)–map
119

Discover Alaska–160

Discovery–25, 101, 153

Disenchantment Bay–10, 130

District of Alaska–170

Dixon, George, explorer–24

dog sledding, dog mushing–
photo 124, 128, 129, 190

Dolly Varden char–18, 77,
130, 140, 189

Dolly's House Museum, former home of Dolly Arthur
(K)–39

Douglas Café–113

Douglas Island–83, 87, 102

Doyle's Boat Rental–184

Drucker, Philip–200

Duncan, William–22-23, 47

dune buggy–43 (K)

Dungeness crabs (J)–101

Dupont (J)–map 10, 87

Dyea (Sk)–map 119, 120,
123, 128

Dyea Campground (Sk)–map
119

Dyea Slide Cemetery (Sk)–photo 126

E

Eagle Center (K)–map 32, 40

Eagle Council Grounds (H)–map 137, photo, 144-145

Eagle Totem (W)–51

Eagles. See bald eagles

Eagle's Roost Park (P)–74

El Capitan Underground Cave Tour–47

Eldred Rock lighthouse–93, 112

Elfin Cove–map 11

emergency help–196

Emmons, George Thornton–28, 200

Equinox Wilderness Expeditions–66

ERA Helicopters–198

Eskimos–101, 165

eulachon. See hooligan

Evergreen Avenue (J)–86

Evergreen Cemetery (J)–map 88

explorers of Southeast Alaska–23-25, 34, 59, 83, 86, 153, 162-163

F

Fairbanks–122

Fairweather Range–160

Falls Creek Fish Ladder (P)–71

Family, The, a modern totem (J)–95

Favorite Channel–86

Ferebee Glacier (Sk)–128

Ferguson, Judy–200

ferry service. See Alaska Fjordlines, Alaska Marine Highway and Chilkat Cruises

festivals and annual events–186-189

Field Guide to Alaskan Wildflowers (Pratt)–201

First Russian Voyage around the World, The: The Journal of Hermann Ludwig von Lowenstern (Moessner, ed.)–200

fish camps–25, 69, 83, 86, 100, 133

Fish Creek (K)–35

fish ladders (K)–39, (P)–78

Fish Pirate's Daughter, The, melodrama featuring local history (K)–41, 188

fish processing. See canneries, fishing industry, salmon

fish traps, ancient Tlingit–74, 76-77, 96

fishing, recreational–43, 46 (K); 78, 81 (P); 101 (J); 130 (Sk); photo 134 (H); 140 (H); 157 (GBNP); 178 (Sit); 185, 189-190

fishing derbies–74, 186, 190

Fishing Hotline–189

fishing industry–64, 65, 73, 77, 102

fishing license–73, 81, 189, 196

Fisk, fountain-sculpture by Carson Aboysen, 1967 (P)–74

Five Finger lighthouse–93

Fjord Flying Service–198

flightseeing–47 (MFNM); 73, 80 (P); 112 (J); 128 (Sk); 157, 160 (GBNP); 185, 190, 195

float plane–photo 38, 46, 110

float trips–148, 149, 184, 192

flume (J)–87

Folk Festival (J)–186

food–122, 127, 142, 149, 165, 190-192

food, Norwegian–72

Forest Service Information Center (J)–180

Fort Selkirk–134

Fort Williamm H. Seward (AKA Port Chilkoot) (H)–, 133, 142

Fort Wrangell–54

Froot Loop Road (P)–69

four house posts (H)–148

Fourth of July celebrations–188

Fox, Gustavus Vasa–28

frybread–165

funicular (K)–40

Future of Ice, The: A Journey into Cold (Ehrlich)–156

F/V Aleutian Ballad–46

G

Gallery Walk–177

Garden City Glasworks–131

Gastineau Channel (J)–83, map 88, 104

Gastineau Channel Historical Society–112

genealogy–97

geography–17-18, 153, 154

geology–88-89, 104, 120, 153, 156, 162

Geology of Southeast Alaska: Rock and Ice in Motion (Stowell)–201

giardia–195

glacial rebound–18

Glacier Bay Cruise Line–198

Glacier Bay Lodge–map 154, 156

Glacier Bay National Park and Preserve–135, 152-161

Glacier Bay National Park Service–156, 160, 199

Glacier Bay Sea Kayaks–160-161

glacier "blue" bear–130

Glacier Gardens Rainforest Adventure (J)–105

glaciers–maps 11, map 15, 18, 102-104 (J), 130 (Sk), 135, 155 (GBNP), map 154, 160, 161, 190

glass blowing–131

global warming–84, 104, 160

gold–9

Gold Belt (J)–83, 88

Gold Creek (J)–86, 105

gold mining–86, 87, 88, 94, 115-123

gold panning–photo 113, 192-193

Gold Rush Cemetery (Sk)–97, 128

gold rushes in Southeast Alaska–35, 88, 121-123, 134

Gold Street (J)–87, 95, 104-105

Goldbelt Tours (J)–110

Golden North Hotel (Sk)–123

"Golden Stairs"–131

golf–65, 186

Gonakadet Totem (W)–64

Governor's House, 1912 (J)–98

Grand Pacific Glacier (GBNP)–153, 161

Gravina Island–30

Gray, Robert–24

Gray Line of Alaska–192

grease (hooligan oil) trails–133-134

Great Alaska Craftbeer & Homebrew Festival (H)–186

Great Alaskan Lumberjack Show (K)–39

green travel–193

Gregg, Mimi and Ted–136, 48

Guide to Marine Mammals of Alaska (Wynne)–201

Gulf of Alaska–maps 10, 15

Gustavus–map 11, 14, 156, 160, 181

Gustavus Visitors Association–160

H

Haa Kusteeyi, Our Culture (Dauenhauer and Dauenhauer)–168

Haida people–19, 23, 24, 162

Haines–132-149, 189

Haines, Francina, Presbyterian fundraiser–134

Haines Convention & Visitors Bureau–142, 199

Haines Highway–133, 146

Haines is for Hikers brochure–146

Haines Junction–133, map 137

halibut–28, 73, 102, 140, 178

Hammer Museum (H)–142

Hammer's Slough Historical Area (P)–map 71, photo 73, 74

Hammond-Wickersham House, 1899 (J)–95

harbor porpoise–160

harbor seals (GBNP)–153, 181

Hard Rock Gold (Stone)–89

Harnessing the Atom totem pole by Amos Wallace (J)–96

Harrigan Centennial Building (Sit)–173

Harris, Richard–87, 88

Harris Aircraft Services Inc. (Sit)–198

Harris and Juneau monument (J)–100

Hegg, Eric A.–121

Heinmiller, Carl–136

Heinmiller, Lee–137

helicopter flightseeing–73 (P), 128 (Sk), 190

hemlock–17, 38, 177

Herbert Glacier (J)–93

herring–21, 162

highliner–70

hiking–65, 80, 87, 101, 104, 105, 131, 148, 160

History and Walking tour of Fort William H. Seward pamphlet–142

history conservation, 137-138, 143, 146, 156; early settlers, 142

History of the Mines and Miners in the Juneau Gold Belt (Redman)–89

Holland America Westours–157, 198

Hollis (POW)–47

Holm, Bill, carver–48

hooligan (AKA eulachon)–21, 66, 134, 148

Hoonah–map 11, 153, 155

hostels–map 119, 194

hot springs (W)–57, 66

Hotel Halsingland (H)–149, 193

hotel rates, off-season–194

hover fly–18

Howard, Cliford–200

Hubbard Glacier–130

Hudson's Bay Company–20, 24, 54, 118

Hummingbird Hollow art gallery (J)–113

humpback whale–14, 57, 73, 74, 75, photo 76, 81, 160, 178

Huna Tlingit–153

Hungry Point View Area (P)–74

Hydaburg–21

hypothermia–195

I

ice. See bergy seltzer, iceworm, glaciers

Icy Bay–66

Icy Strait (GBNP)–157

Icy Strait Point –189

Icy Straits Packing Company (P)–69

Indian River (Sit)–map 164

Inside Passage–9, 10, map 11, 25, 78, 93, 115, 133, 147, 185, 189, 191

Inside Passage: Living with Killer Whales, Bald Eagles, and Kwakiutl Indians (Modzelewski)–78

Institute Creek Trail (W)–65

Inter-Island Ferry Authority (POW, W)–198

Internet access (P)–73

Irene Ingle Public Library (W)–64

ivory–131

J

J. M. Davis House (J)–95

Jackson, Nathan, master carver (K)–48

Jackson, Norman, master carver (K)–48

Jackson, Sheldon, missionary/educator–176

James and Elsie Nolan Civic Center/Wrangell Museum (W)–58

Japonski Island (Sit)–170

jet boat tours–185

Jettmar, Karen, guide–66

Jewell Gardens (Sk)–127

John Rishel Mineral Information Center (J)–105, 110

Johns Hopkins Glacier (GBNP)–153

Jones, James Earl–135

Journeys to Alaska (Scidmore)–44

Juneau–44, 82-113, 181

Juneau, Joe–87, 88

Juneau Convention & Visitors Bureau–199

Juneau-Douglas City Museum (J)–96, 97, 98

Juneau Ice Field–84, 93, 129, 190

Juneau Parks and Recreation Department–105

JuneauAlaska.com–199

Junior Ranger Program–171

K

Kadjisdu.axtc (carver)–148

Kake Island–56

Kanaut, Stikine Tlingit chief–34

Katlian, Tlingit war leader–163, 166, 176

Katzeek, John–148

kayak adventures–41 (K), 73, 81 (P), 103, 105 (J), 148 (H), 157, 160-161 (GBNP), 178 (Sit)

Keet Gooshi Tours (H)–148

Kenai–83

Ketchikan–18, 30-49, 177

Ketchikan Air–198

Ketchikan Carver–48

Ketchikan Coffee Company–49

Ketchikan Ranger District/Misty Fiords National Monument–199

Ketchikan Reservation Service–194

Ketchikan Visitors Bureau–38, 199

Khlebnikov, Andrei, navigator–24

Kid Stuff–16, 39 (K), 57 (W), 77 (P), 101 (J), 127 (Sk), 143 (H), 171 (Sit)

Kiks.adi Tlingit–162, 163, 168

Kiksetti Totem Park–63

killer whale–35, 74, 148, 161

Killer Whale Fin House (H)–148

Killisnoo–map 11

Kinder Komfort (P)–77

King Salmon Derby–74

Kito's Cave (P)–74

Klehini River–143

Klondike Gold Rush–9, 97, 115, 120-123

Klondike Gold Rush, The: Photographs from 1896-1899 (Wilson)–201

Klondike Gold Rush National Historic Park (Sk and Seattle)–119, 126, 127

Klondike Gold Rush National Historic Park Visitor Center (Sk)–199

Klondike Rainforest bike tour–193

Klondike Road Race (Sk)–188

Kluane National Park & Reserve (Canada)–map 11, 133, 149

Kluane to Chilkat Bike Relay (H)–186, 188

Klukwan–map 11, 98, 128, 148

Kodiak–26, 83, 168

Kodiak Island–18

Kolosh, Russian name for the people–20, 162

Konstantinovsk–28

Kowee, Chief–88, 100

Kroschel Park wildlife sanctuary (H)–143

Kupreanof, Ivan Antonovich–69

Kupreanof Flying Service–198

Kupreanof Island (P)–69

Kwakiutl people–19

L

L.A.B. Flying Service, Inc.–160, 190, 198

Lake Bennett–126

land–17-18

Last Chance Basin (J)–87

Last Chance Mining Museum & Historical Park (J)–87, 104

Last New Land, The: Stories of Alaska, Past and Present (Mergler, ed.)–200

Laughton Glacier (Sk)–129

LeConte Glacier (P)–69, 80, 190

Lee's Clothing (P)–81

Leikarring Dancers (P)–72

Lemesurier Island (GBNP)–map 154

Lemon Creek (J)–map 85

Lende, Heather–138

Lewis Building, 1896 (J)–98

Libby, McNeill, and Libby Cannery (K)–43

libraries (P)–73

lichen (moss)–19, 78

Lighthouse Cruise & Keeper's Lunch (J)–112

lighthouses–93, 112

Linblad Expeditions–198

Lincoln–45

Lincoln Street (Sit)–map 164, 172

ling cod–178

Lisiansky, Iurii (Urey) Fedorovich–24, 166

Little Ice Age–18, 153

Little Norway, nickname for Petersburg–72

Little Norway Festival (P)–72, 74

Lituya Bay–25

lodging–193-194

logging. See timber industry

logging demonstrations–39, 188

London, Jack–115, 118, 200

Loop Trail in Volunteer Park (W)–map 52

Lost Heritage of Alaska, The: Adventures and Art of the Alaskan Coastal Indians (Miller and Miller)–55

Ludvig's Bistro (Sit)–179

Lynn Canal–83, 88, 105, 115, 133, 135

lynx–177

M

Made in Alaska certification–194

Majestic America Line–198

maps–11, 15, 32, 52, 71, 85, 88, 119, 137, 154, 164

Marchand, Etienne–24

Margerie Glacier (GBNP)–157, 161

Marine Park (J)–96

marmots–101

Married Man's Trail (K)–39

Martha Black: Her Story from the Dawson Gold Fields to the Halls of Parliament (Whyard ed.)–122

Martin, Mike–34-35

Mary Island lighthouse–93

Mascot Saloon (Sk)–photo 119

masks–113, 141

Matanuska Colony–97

McFarland, Amanda–56

Meares, John–24

Mendenhall Glacier (J)–84, 93, 102-103, photo 104

Mendenhall Golf Course (J)–186

Mendenhall River (J)–192

Mendenhall Valley (J)–92

Mendenhall Wetlands (J)–map 85, 105

Mergler, Wayne–200

Metlakatla–22, 47

minerals–105, 110, 123, 136, 183. See also gold

mining tour–104

missionaries–56, 59, 134, 167

Misty Fiords National Monument–30, 42, 46-47

Mitkof Island, 211 square miles on east shore of Wrangell Narrows; site of Petersburg–69

Moessner, Victoria Joan–200

moieties–21, 176

Monrean House (K)–41

Montana Creek (J)–83

Moore, William, founder of Skagway–115, 118, 120

moose–66, 143, 161, 182-183

Moraine Ecology Trail (J)–104

Mosquito Lake State Recreation Site (H)–140

Mosquito Legend totem pole (J)–98

moss–78

Mount Crillon (GBNP)–160

Mount Dewey (W)–64

Mount Edgecumbe (Sit)–162, 174-175

Mount Fairweather–160

Mount Juneau (J)–92

Mount Juneau Trading Post–113

Mount Riley (H)–146, 148

Mount Roberts (J)–82, 84, 101

Mount Roberts Trail (J)–101

Mount Roberts Tramway (J)–photo 82, 96, 101

mountain goat–102,(photo 183)–183

Mountain Market (H)–149

MS Sheltered Seas–58

Muir, John, naturalist/ author–56, 118, 134, 153, 200

Muir Glacier (GBNP)–map 154

Muir Inlet (GBNP)–map 154

music festivals–186

muskeg–69, 80

Muskeg Meadows Golf Course and Shooting Range (W)–map 52, 65

N

names of chiefs, traditional–21

names of plank houses, traditional–21

National Park Service–123, 156

National Recreation Reservation Service–80

National Register of Historic Places–94, 104

National Weather Service–196

Native Alaskans–19-21, 100, 170

Native art–194

Native traditions–21-23

natural resources–9, 18, 21, 162, 177

Nature of Southeast Alaska, The (O'Clair, Armstrong and Carstensen)–200

Neva warship–166

New Archangel–166

New Eddystone Rock (MFNM)–42

Nome–122

Nootka–21

Nootka Sound, British Columbia–141

Norquest Seafoods Cannery (P)–72, 73

Norris Gift Shop–66

North Douglas boat ramp (J)–105

Northwest Coast art revival–142

Northwest Passage–83

Northwestern American Company–25

Norwegian Cruise Lines–198

Nugget Falls (J)–104

O

O'Clair, Rita–200

O'Connell Bridge (Sit)–172

Old Witch Totem Pole carved by Dwight Wallace, c. 1880 (J)–96

Oliver, Marvin (K)–48

On Your Knees Cave (POW)–30

Ononnistoy, Stikine Tlingit chief–35

orca, AKA killer whale–74, 75, 153, 160, 161

Ordonez, Joe–143

Oseakken, Willis–179

"Outside"–53

P

Pacific Coast & Norway Packing (P)–69

Pacific Coast Steamship Co.–44, 121-122

Pacific Fur Company–167

Pacific Wing Air Charters–198

Pack Creek–110

Packer Expeditions (Sk)–129, 130

Palin, Governor Sarah–29

Pan American Airways–38

Paper Nose Charlie–35

"Paris of the North Pacific" (Sitka)–165

Parnassus Books (K)–39

Pascol, Dwayne, carver–48

Patsy Ann bronze sculpture by Anna Burke Harris 1992 (J)–95

Pelican–map 11

Perez, Juan–23, 162

Perseverance Trail (J)–87

Petersburg–68-81

Petersburg Gallery Walk–188

Petersburg Medical Center (P)–73

Petersburg Ranger District–80

Petersburg Vacations–73

Petersburg Visitor Information Center–74, 199

Petroglyph Beach State Historic Park (W)–57, 60-61, 64

petroglyphs–57 (W), 76-77 (P), 183

phone numbers–196-199

phratries–21

plank houses–21

plant succession as glaciers retreat–157, 160

Pleasant Camp, Canada (H)–149

Point Adolphus–160

Point Retreat lighthouse–93, 112

Polar Bear Dip (J)–186

Pook, Cathleen–179

Porcupine–136

Porcupine Gold bike tour–193

Port Chilkoot Dock (H)–map 136, 142

Portage Cove (H)–133, photo 140

Portage Cove Campground (H)–map 137

Portlock, Nathaniel, Lieutenant–23-24

potlatch–21-22; photo 166; suppression of, 167; 178

Pratt, Verna E.–201

Price, Wayne, carver–48

prices–191

Prince of Wales Island–, 20, 30, 188

Prince William Sound–18, 25, 83, 162

Princess Cruises–198

Princess Tours–104, 157

Promech Air (K)–198

promyshlenniki–9

Pullen Creek RV Park (Sk)–map 119

pulp, wood–70

Pyles' Dockside Gallery–43

Pyramid Harbor (H)–134

Q

Queen Charlotte Islands, Canada–163

R

Radisson Seven Seas Cruises–198

rain fall–17-18, 72-73, 83, 84, 126, 133, 160, 185

rain forest–17-18, 105, 138, 185

Rainbow Falls Trail (W)–65

Rainbow Glacier–135

rainbow trout (K)–40

Rainwalker Expeditions (W)–65

Rainy Hollow (H)–136

Raptor Center (J)–map 85

raven–66, 147

Raven legends–98-99

Raven's Journey art gallery (J)–113

recommended reading—200-201

Red Dog Saloon (J)–photo 99

Red Onion Saloon (Sk)–photo 129

Redoubt Saint Dionysius–54

Regat, Jacques and Mary–179

Reid, Frank–123

Revillagigedo Island (TNF)–34

Rezanov, Nikolai–24

Riggs Glacier (GBNP)–map 154

river otter–47, 105, 177

river rafting–185

Roll On! Discovering the Wild Stikine River (Demerjian)–200

rookeries, bird–70, 161

Rooney's Northern Lights Restaurant (P)–81

Roosevelt, Pres. Theodore–29

rosemaling (P)–72, 74, photo 78

Royal Canadian Mounted Police–97, 121, 149

Royal Caribbean Cruise Line–198

rubbings of petroglyphs–57

Russell Fiord–130

Russell Island (GBNP)–map 154

Russian America 1741-1867–9, 100

Russian-American Company–9, 24, 25, 54, 69, 162, 173, 178

Russian Bishop's House (Sit)–map 164, 173

Russian blockhouse replica (Sit)–map 164

Russian explorers–9, 25-28, 162-163

Russian Orthodox Church (Sit)–162

RV parks–194

S

Saginaw–56

sailboat race–185

St. Elias Mountains (GBNP)–149, 156

St. Michael's Cathedral (Sit)–172, 178

St. Nicholas Russian Orthodox Church (J)–95

St. Peter's by-the-sea Episcopal Church (Sit)–map 164

St. Rose of Lima Catholic Church (W)–64

Salish people–19

salmon–21, 33, 35, 53, 65, 69, 73, 80, 130, 134, 140, photo 146, 178

Salmon Landing Market (K)–, map 32, 48

Sandpiper Café–113

Sandy Beach (J)–111

Sawyer Glaciers–110

Saxman, Samuel–34

Saxman Arts Co-op (K)–47-48

Saxman Village (K)–34, 39, 43, 98

Saxman Village Store–47

Saxman Village Totem Park (K)–45

Schoenbar Trail (K)–map 32

scrimshaw–131

sea cucumber–73

sea lion–81, 130, 158-159, 162, 178

sea otter–9, 25, 162, 178

seafood–72, 73, 77, 110, 160, 191

Seahorse Ventures–41, 43

Sealife Discovery Tours (Sit)–178

Sealing Cove (Sit)–map 164

seals–110, 130, 181

Seawold/Whale Rider gallery (H)–149

"Seeing Daylight" (film about Tlingit culture) (J)–101

Sentinel Island lighthouse–93, 112

Seward, William H., U. S. Secretary of State–28, 133, 134, 170

"Seward's Ice Box "–44, 170

Shady Lady Fancy Dress Ball–186

Shakes, as a traditional name for a Tlingit chief–21, 54

Shakes Island (W)–50, 63

Shakes V–55

Shakes VI–64

Shakes VII–58

Shakes Tribal House–58

Shapes of Their Thoughts: Reflections of Culture Contact in Northwest

Coast Indian Art (Wyatt)–167

Sheep Creek Mine (J)–95

Sheet'ka Kwaan Naa Kahidi Tribal House (Sit)–176, 178

Sheldon, Steve and Elisabeth–142

Sheldon Jackson College (Sit)–map 164, 176

Sheldon Jackson Museum (Sit)–map 164, 176, 178

Sheldon Museum and Cultural Center (H)–142

Shelikov, Natalia–25

shellfish farming–38

shipping art home–194

Shoemaker Overlook (W)–65

shooting range, Muskeg Meadows (W)–52

shopping cautions–194

shopping recommendations–178-179, 194

shoulder season–126-127

shrew–18

shrimp–50, 72

Shustaks, a Stikine chief–56

Silver Bow Basin (J)–87, 88

Silver Hand tag of authenticity–194

Simpson, George–24

Sing Lee Alley (P)–74

Sing Lee Alley Boosk (P)–74

Sitka–9, 25, 92, 162-179, map 163

Sitka black-tailed deer. See deer, Sitka black-tailed

Sitka Convention & Visitors Bureau–173, 199

Sitka Historical Museum (Sit)–173

Sitka National Cemetery (Sit)–map 164

Sitka National Historical Park (Sit)–map 164, 171, 176

Sitka National Monument–170

Sitka Rose Gallery (Sit)–178

Sitka Sound (Sit)–map 162, 164

Sitka spruce–18, 157, 177

Skaguay News–121

Skagway–84, 115-131, map 119

Skagway Brewing Co. (Sk)– map 119

Skagway Convention & Visitors Bureau–199

Skagway Inn Bed & Breakfast (1897) (Sk)–map 119, 127

Skagway Museum & Archive (Sk)–, 97, 128

Skagway River (Sk)–115, map 119, 127

Skagway Story, The (Clifford)–200

Skayeutlelt, Tlingit chief–162, 163

Skookum Jim–115

Slide Cemetery (Sk)–photo 126

slime line–77, photo 80

smallpox–9, 20, 24, 54, 168

Smith, Jefferson Randolph "Soapy," con man–120, 121, 123

Sockeye Cycle–193

Snow Dragon Parade (H)–189

Soapy Smith's Parlor (Sk)– map 119

Sons of Norway Hall (P)–photo 70, 74

South Marble Island (GBNP)–photo 158-159

Southeast Alaska Discovery Center (K)–map 32, 45

Southeast Alaska Fairgrounds (H)–148

Southeast Alaska Indian Cultural Center (Sit)–176

Southeast Alaska State Fairgrounds (H)–143, 148

Southeast Alaska Tourism Council–199

Southeast Sea Kayaks–41, 47

spawning salmon–39 (K), 82 (J), 101 (J) 138 (H)

spelunking (POW)–47

Spirit of Adventure–161

sports–148, 186-187

Spruce Mill Mall (K)–48

squirrel–177

Stan Price State Wildlife Sanctuary (Pack Creek)– 180

Stanford, Susan–179

State Capitol Building (J)–map 88

State Office Building (J)–map 88, 96

steamship menu–26

steamships–9, 56, 72, 92, 121-122, 177

Steele, Samuel–121

Steller sea lions–photo 158-159, 160, 178, 181

Stephens Passage, an 80-mile waterway connecting Frederick Sound and Lynn Canal, bordered on the west by Admiralty Island and on the east by the Alaska mainland and Douglas Island–75, 93

stickleback–18

Stickeen Glacier–44

Stickeen people–50

Stikine-LeConte Wilderness (W)–66

Stikine River–50

Stowaway Café (Sk)–131

Stowel, Harold H.–201

Strong, Annie Hall–121

Stroud, Robert, the "birdman of Alcatraz"–94

Sumdum–110

Sunrise Aviation (W)–198

survival along the Inside Passage–195

Swan Lake (Sit)–168

Swan Observatory (P)–76

swans–76

Syttende Mai–72

T

Tagook, Charlie–98

Taku Fisheries Ice House (J)–102

Taku Glacier–92

Taku Glacier Lodge (J)–110

Taku Tlingit–83

TEMSCO Helicopters (W, J, Sk)–190

Tent City Days (W)–186

terns–104

Thane Ore House Salmon Bake (J)–113

Thundering Wings Eagle Park (K)–map 32

tidewater glacier trip (GBNP)–161

timber industry–38, 56, 62, 136, 167, 177

Timberline Bar & Grill, theater/nature center–101

time–195, 196

Tina's Kitchen –81

Tlingit art–148

Tlingit culture–136-137

Tlingit Indians, The (Emmons and de Laguna)–200

Tlingit people–9, 19, 50, 54, 133, 142, 172

Tlingit prehistory–50, 54, 76, 83, 162

Tlingit words–33, 86, 118, 147, 148, 153, 172

Tom Pittman Geology and Mining Museum (J)–110

Tongass Historical Museum (K)–39

Tongass Kayak Adventures (P)–81

Tongass Narrows–10, 30

Tongass National Forest–80, 105, 138, 176, 199

Tonka Seafoods (P)–77

Totem Bight State Historical Park (K)–photo 46, 192

totem carving workshop (H)–59

Totem Heritage Cultural Center (K)–40

totem poles–22, 38-39, photos 40-41, 46 (K), photo 51, 55, 59 (W), 94, 96, 98 (J), 142 (H), photos 150-151

Totem Square (Sit)–map 164

tourism–38, 44, 72, 92, 115, 123, 160, 177

tracing gold rush ancestors–97

Tracy Arm Fjord (TNF)–photo 106-107, 110, 185

trade–21-22, 24, 26, 54, 100, 133, 141, 162, 173

trading posts–123, photo 136

Traditional Knowledge Camp (H)–148

Trail Mix (J)–105

Trail of '98 Museum (Sk)–128

Trail of Time (J)–104

trails. See hiking or specific trail names

transportation–191-192

travel industry information–199

Travels in Alaska (Muir; Hoagland, intro.)–200

Treadwell, John–111

Treadwell Complex gold mines (J)–89, 94, 111

Treadwell Ditch (J)–111

Treadwell Historic Trail (J)–87, 111

Tree Point lighthouse–93

Tribal House of the Bear (W)–63-64

Troll, Ray–48

Tsimshian people–19, 28, 47

Tsirku Canning Company Museum (H)–142

Tsirku River (H)–143

TTY–199

U

U.S. Coast Guard, 17th District–87, 170, 196

U. S. currency–53

U.S. Customs–196

U.S. Forest Service–110, 112, 177, 180, 194

U.S. Forest Service Ranger Station (W)–65

Unalaska–83

underwater exploration (Sit)–178

University of Alaska Southeast (J)–92

V

Vancouver, Captain George, explorer–23, 25, 34, 69, 83, 86, 141, 153

Vanderbuilt Reef–112

Veniaminov, Bishop Ivan– 168, 172, 173

Victoria, British Columbia–24, 56

Viking Bar (J)–96

Viking ship replica (P)–(photo) 72

Viking Travel–81

visitor information–199

volcanoes, volcanic activity– photo 42, 174-175

von Wrangel, Baron Ferdinand–54

W

Wacky & Wonderful Roadside Attractions of Alaska (Walker)–102

Walker-Broderick House (K)–41

Wallace, Amos, Tlingit carver and silversmith–96

walrus ivory–131

Ward Air Inc. (J)–198

Ward Cove pulp mill (K)–38

weather of Southeast Alaska–72-73, 80, 126, 133, 160, 195

web sites–listed throughout the volume and 199

Welcome Totems Park (H)–142

West Coast Cape Fox Lodge (K)–40, 48-49

Westmark Sitka (Sit)–179

Whale Observatory (P)–74

Whale Park (K)–38-39

Whale Park (Sit)–map 164

Whale Song Cruises (P)–81

whales–47 (K), 53 (W), 73, 74, 81 (P) 160, 161 (GBNP), 162 (Sit), 181

Whidby, Joseph–83

White Pass & Yukon Railroad Depot (Sk)–127

White Pass & Yukon Route (Sk)–121, 126, 129

White Pass Trail (Sk)–115, 118, 126

White Pass Train and bike tour–193

White Run (H)–136

Whitehorse, Yukon Territory–97, 115

Whitepass Steamship Line–90

Wickersham House (J)–95

Wickersham, Judge James–29, 95

Wild Celery (shop) (P)–81

wildlife viewing. See birds and specific animals

William Moore Cabin (1887) (Sk)–map 119, 123

William Winn/Bell House (J)–94

Willoughby Avenue (J)–100

Wilson, Graham–201

Windfall Fisherman cast bronze sculpture by R. T. Wallen (J)–95

Wings Airways–110

Wings of Alaska Airlines–112, 198

winter activities, events–186, 187-188

Winter Arts Faire (K)–43

Wisconsin glaciation–18

Wolf 18 (Shakes V)–55

World Heritage Site–156

World War I–44

World War II–89, 123, 136, 170, 177

World's Columbian Exposition, Chicago, 1893–59

wolverine–18, 148, 177

wolves–83, 143

Wrangell–50-67, 93

Wrangell Chamber of Commerce–58

Wrangell Community Church of God–57

Wrangell Island–54

Wrangell Museum (W)–58, 62

Wrangell Narrows, 24-mile waterway connecting Sumner Strait and Frederick Sound and separating Mitkof Island from Kupreanof Island–93

Wrangell Ranger District–66

Wrangell/St. Elias National Park–66

Wrangell Sentinel–56

Wrangell Visitor Information–199

Wynne, Kate–201

Y

Yakutat–map 11, 28, 130

Yakutat Bay–map 10, 20

Yakutat Coastal Airlines–198

Yosemite Glacier–44

Young, S. Hall–56, 134

Yukon & Alaska Genealogy Center–97

Yukon Territory of Canada–map 11, 130, 133

Z

Zak's Café–67

Zarembo, Dionysius Fedorovich–54

Zen restaurant–113

Zerbetz, Evon–48

Zimovia Strait (W)–map 50, 65

zipline tour–102

C O M P A S S
A M E R I C A N   G U I D E S

Critics, booksellers, and travelers all agree: you're lost without a Compass.

"This splendid series provides exactly the sort of historical and cultural detail about North American destinations that curious-minded travelers need."
—*Washington Post*

"This is a series that constantly stuns us . . . no guide with photos this good should have writing this good. But it does."
—*New York Daily News*

"Of the many guidebooks on the market, few are as visually stimulating, as thoroughly researched, or as lively written as the Compass American Guide series."
—*Chicago Tribune*

"Good to read ahead of time, then take along so you don't miss anything."
—*San Diego Magazine*

"Magnificent photography. First rate." —*Money*

"Written by longtime residents of each destination . . . these handsome and literate guides are strong on history and culture, and illustrated with gorgeous photos." —*San Francisco Chronicle*

"The color photographs sparkle, the archival illustrations illuminate windows to the past, and the writing is usually of the utmost caliber."
—*Michigan Tribune*

"Class acts, worth reading and shelving for keeps even if you're not a traveler. "
—*New Orleans Times-Picayune*

"Beautiful photographs and literate writing are the hallmarks of the Compass guides." —*Nashville Tennessean*

"History, geography, and wanderlust converge in these well-conceived books."
—*Raleigh News & Observer*

"Oh, my goodness! What a gorgeous series this is." —*Booklist*

ACKNOWLEDGMENTS

FROM THE AUTHOR AND PHOTOGRAPHER

Ann Chandonnet wishes to thank Ellen Carrlee, Curator of Collections and Exhibits at the Juneau-Douglas City Museum, and Steve Henrikson, Curator of the Alaska State Museum in Juneau, for their generous and enthusiastic help. She is also grateful to the staffs of other museums and visitor centers throughout Southeast Alaska for their invaluable aid in compiling and sorting through material for this book. Without the expertise of individuals like Dragon London of the Ketchikan Visitors Bureau, Heather Marvelle of Baranof Excursions, Michael Naab of the Tongass Historical Museum, John Brower of Klukwan, Chuck Parsley of the Petersburg Ranger District, and Tricia Dindinger of the Juneau Chamber of Commerce, it would be impossible to encapsulate the varied history and scenic glories of the Inside Passage. Further thanks to Don Pitcher for laboring in the mines (literally) to capture unique angles of the northern landscape.

Don Pitcher would like to thank the following people for their assistance in photographing this book: David Allen and Joanne Witta from Goldbelt, Inc.; Michael Brandt from White Pass & Yukon Route Railway; Jim Collins from Allen Marine Tours; Steve Halloran from Glacier Bay Lodge & Tours; Len Lawrence from Inter-Island Ferry Authority; and Kathryn "Ryn" Schneider from Alaska Island Hostel.

FROM THE PUBLISHER

Compass American Guides would like to thank the following individuals or institutions for the use of their illustrations or photographs:
All photographs in this book are by Don Pitcher unless noted below.
Introduction:
Page 10, National Archives and Records Administration
The Land and the People:
Page 16, Museum of History and Industry, Seattle
Page 20, Alaska State Library
Page 24, Barry J. McWayne/University of Alaska Museum of the North (UA69-061-0001)

ABOUT THE AUTHOR

Ann Chandonnet has written extensively on lifestyles, food, arts, and culture for newspapers and magazines on the West Coast. She lived in Alaska for more than 33 years—residing first in Kodiak, then in Chugiak, Anchorage, and finally Juneau from 1999 to 2006. With her husband Fernand, Ann has explored the state on foot and snowshoes as well as by plane, helicopter, ferry, canoe, kayak, and fishing boat. The couple celebrated their 30th anniversary on the Chilkoot Trail. Ann is the author of more than a dozen books, including the prize-winning *Alaska Heritage Seafood Cookbook, Alaska's Arts, Crafts & Collectibles,* and a food history, *Gold Rush Grub: From Turpentine Stew to Hoochinoo.* She was the key-note speaker at the 2007 Alaska Historical Society Conference in Homer. Since retiring to North Carolina, she has learned how to sweat, tickle granddaughters, and raise tomatoes.

ABOUT THE PHOTOGRAPHER

After receiving a master's degree in fire ecology from the University of California at Berkeley, **Don Pitcher** spent 15 summers in the wilds of Alaska and Wyoming. His assignments encompassed everything from mapping grizzly habitat to operating salmon weirs—anything to avoid an office job. He now works as a photographer and travel writer, plotting his travels from Homer, Alaska, where he lives with his wife Karen Shemet and their children Aziza and Rio. Pitcher also photographed the Compass guide to Wyoming, and is the author of comprehensive travel guides for Alaska, Wyoming, Washington, Yellowstone, and the San Juan Islands. His images have appeared in a multitude of other publications and advertisements, and his prints are available in Alaskan galleries. Find details on his latest projects at www.donpitcher.com.